AF225797

Yarn

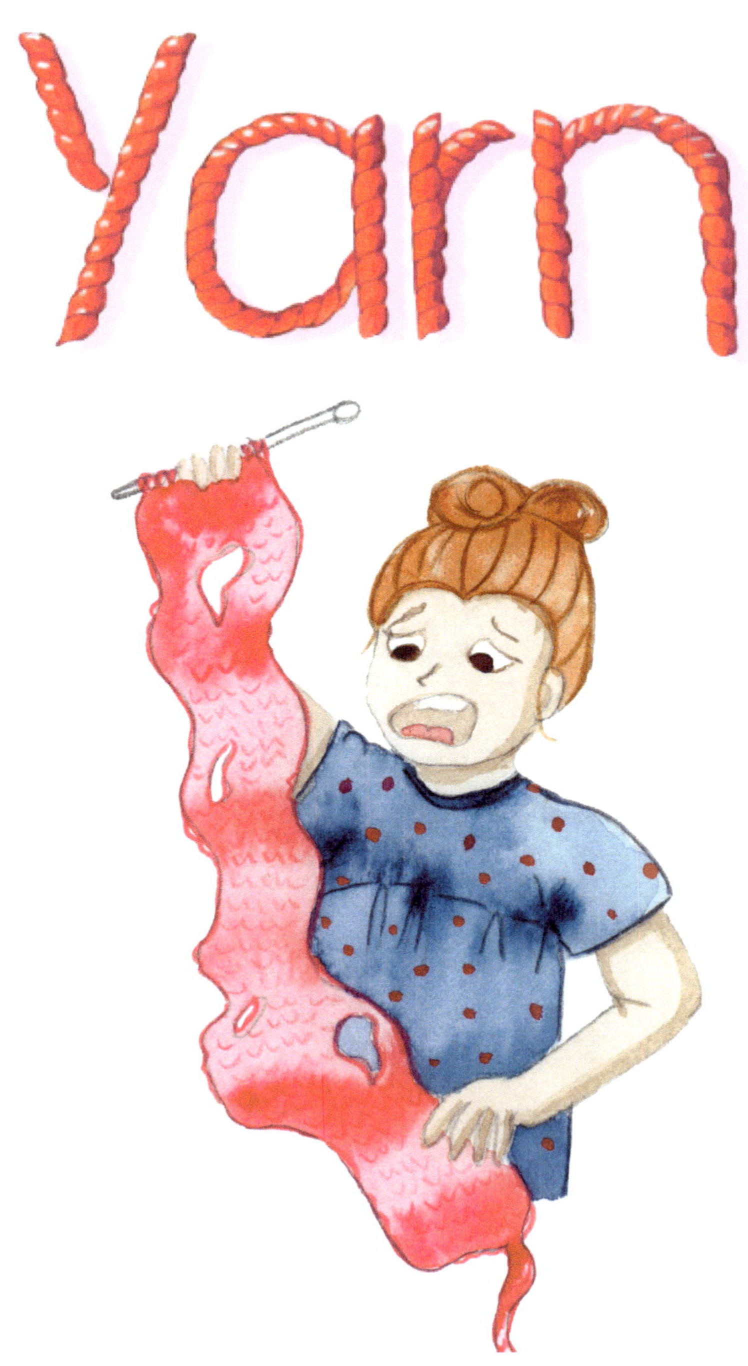

Christine Titheradge   Yvonne Mes

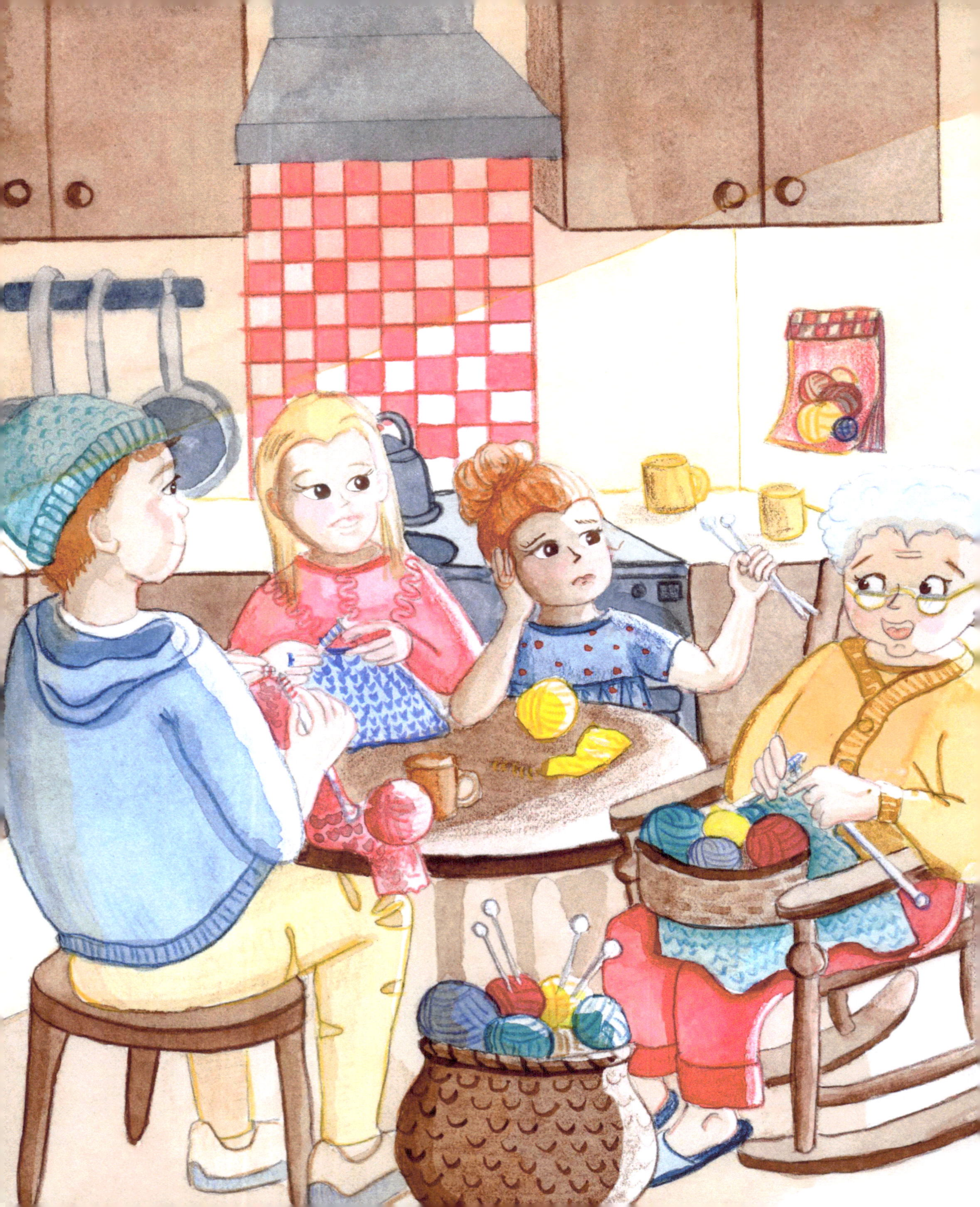

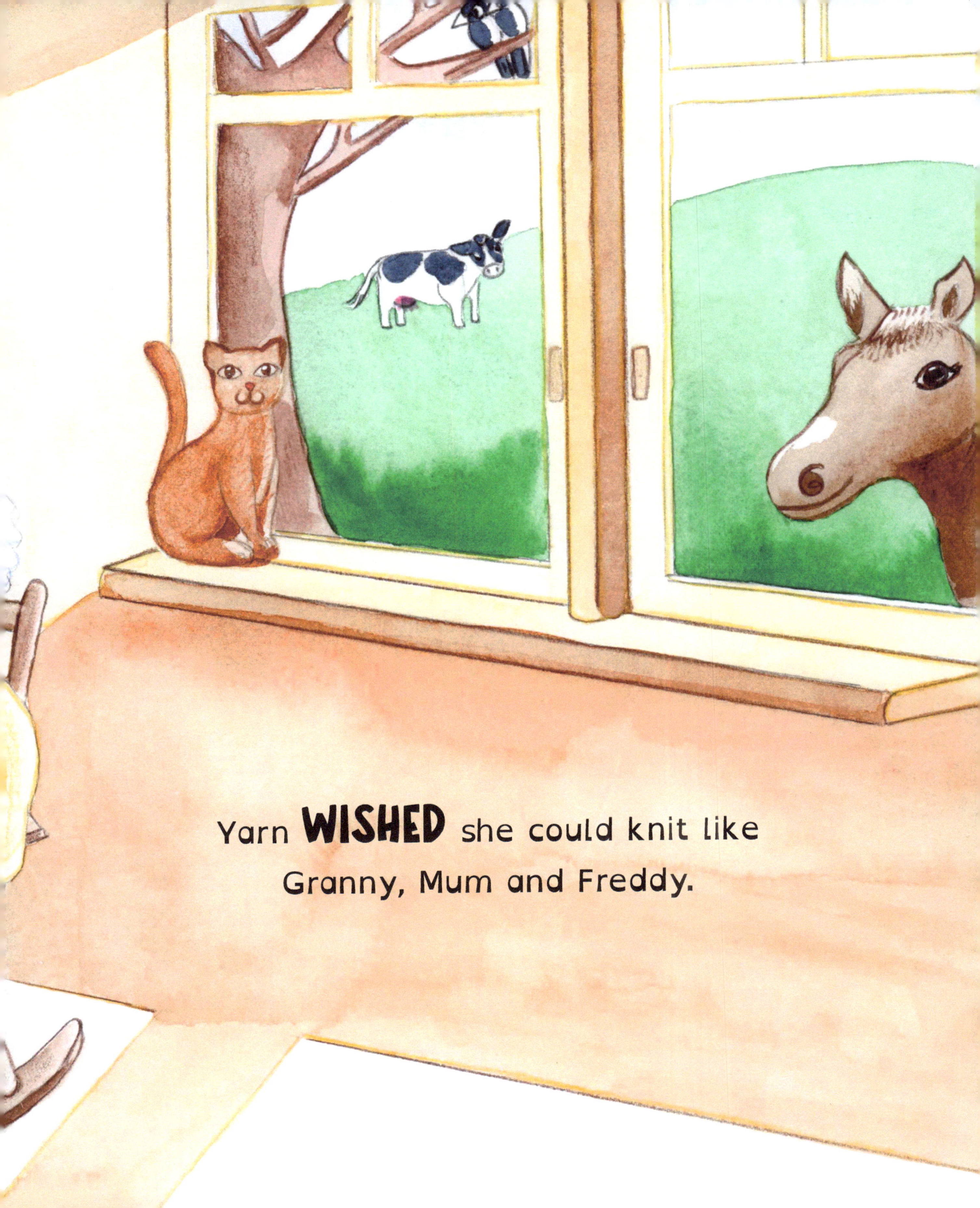

Yarn **WISHED** she could knit like
Granny, Mum and Freddy.

'Try a scarf,' said Granny.
'It's **EASY**,' said Granny.

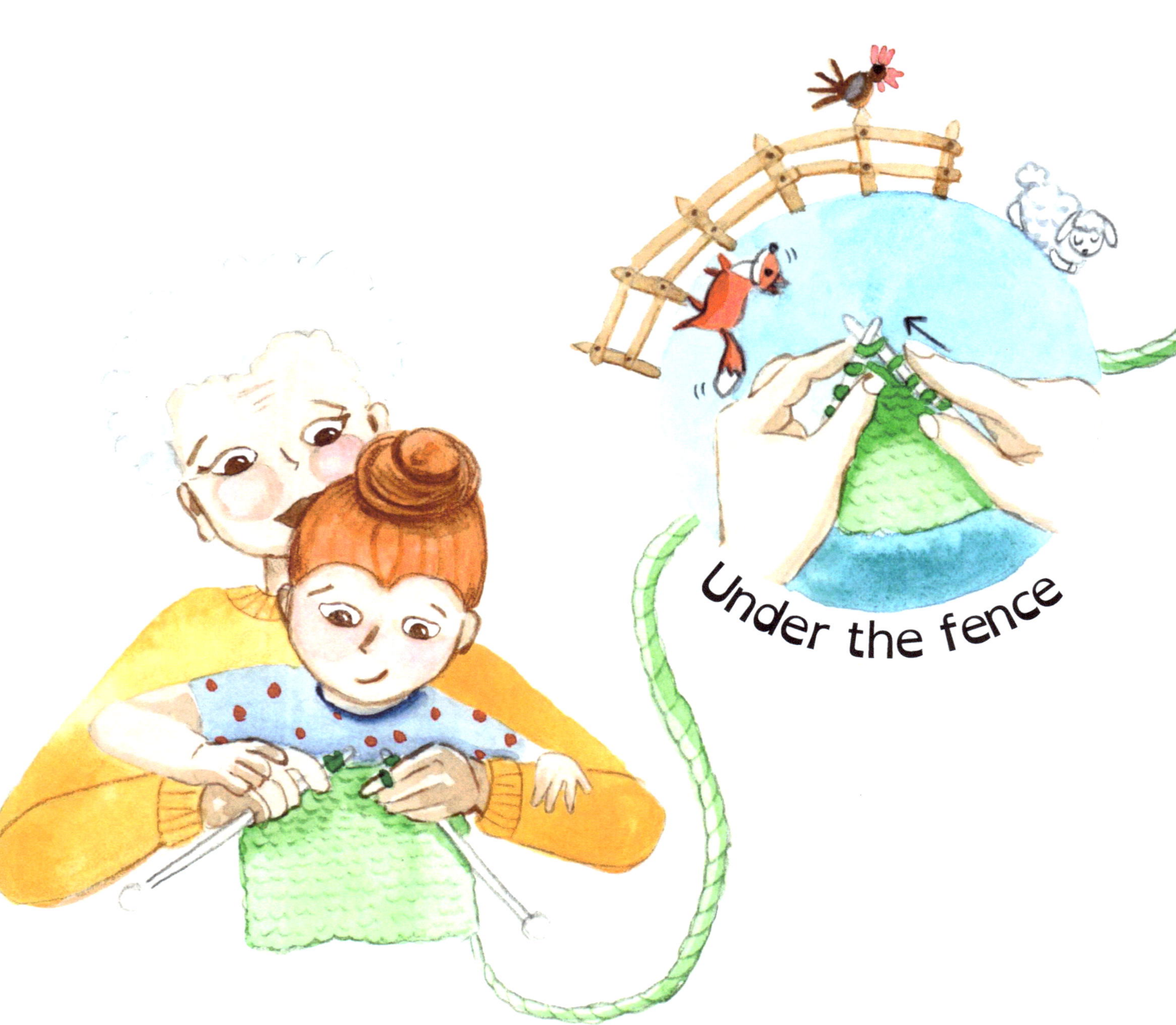

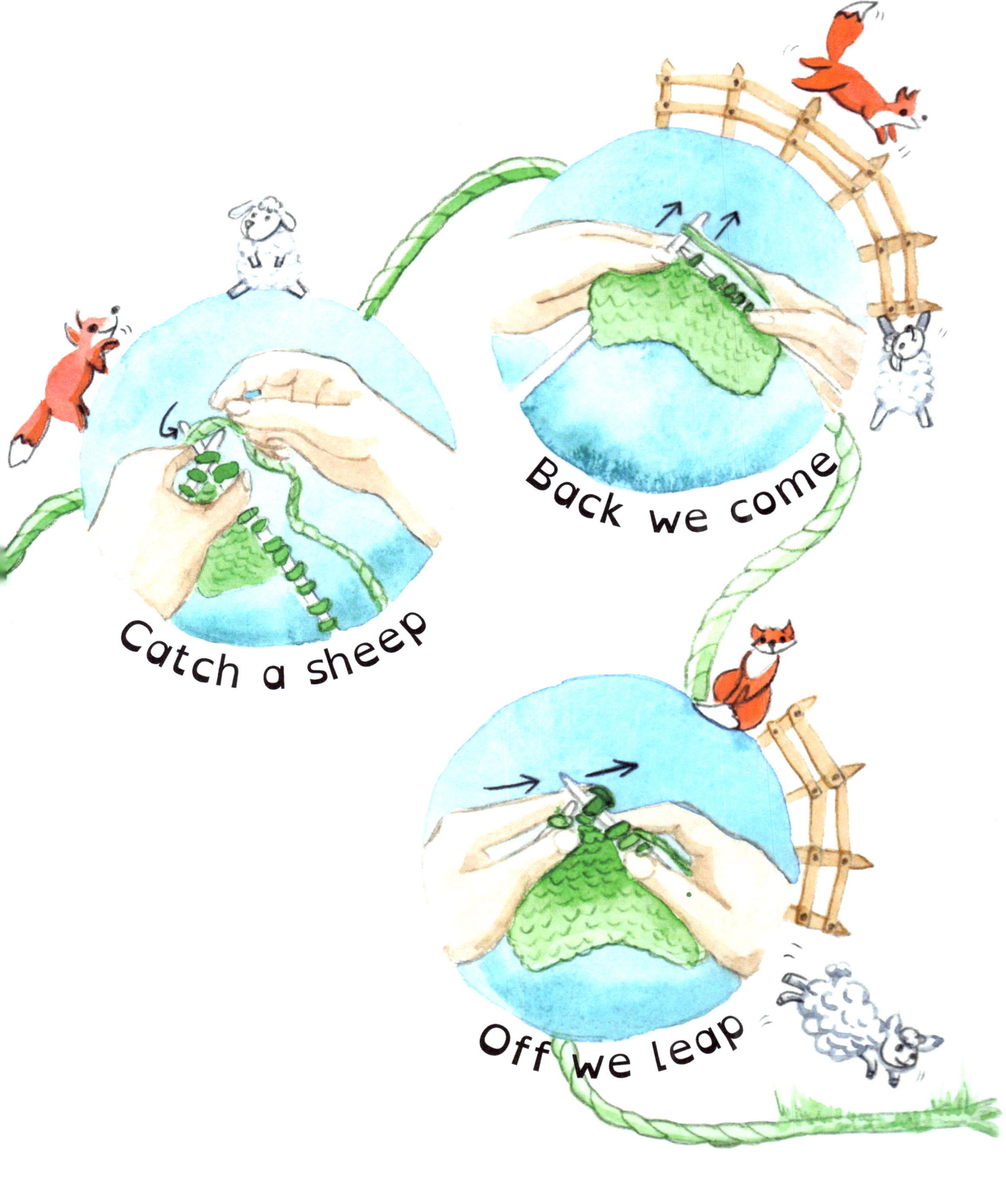

Catch a sheep
Back we come
Off we leap

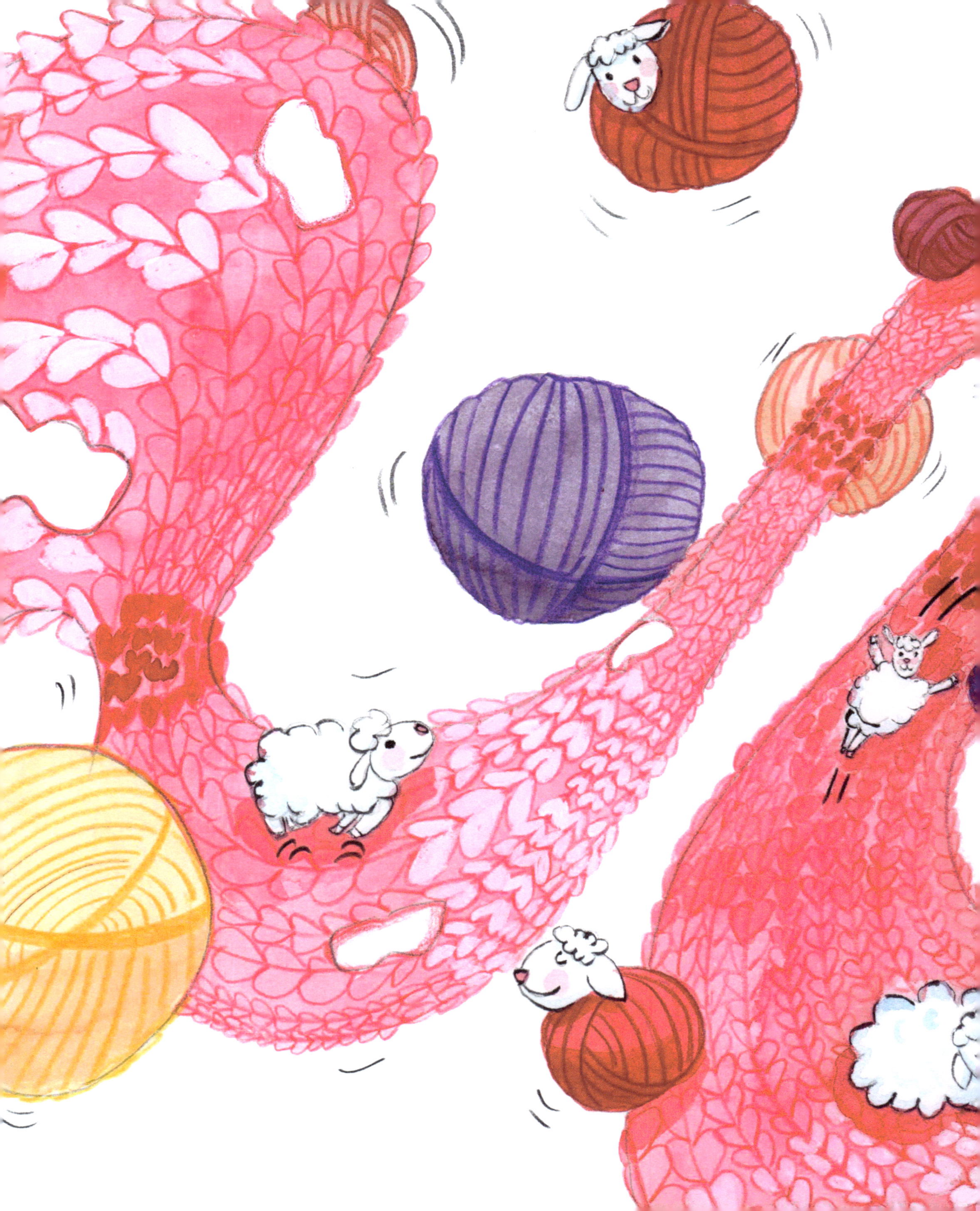

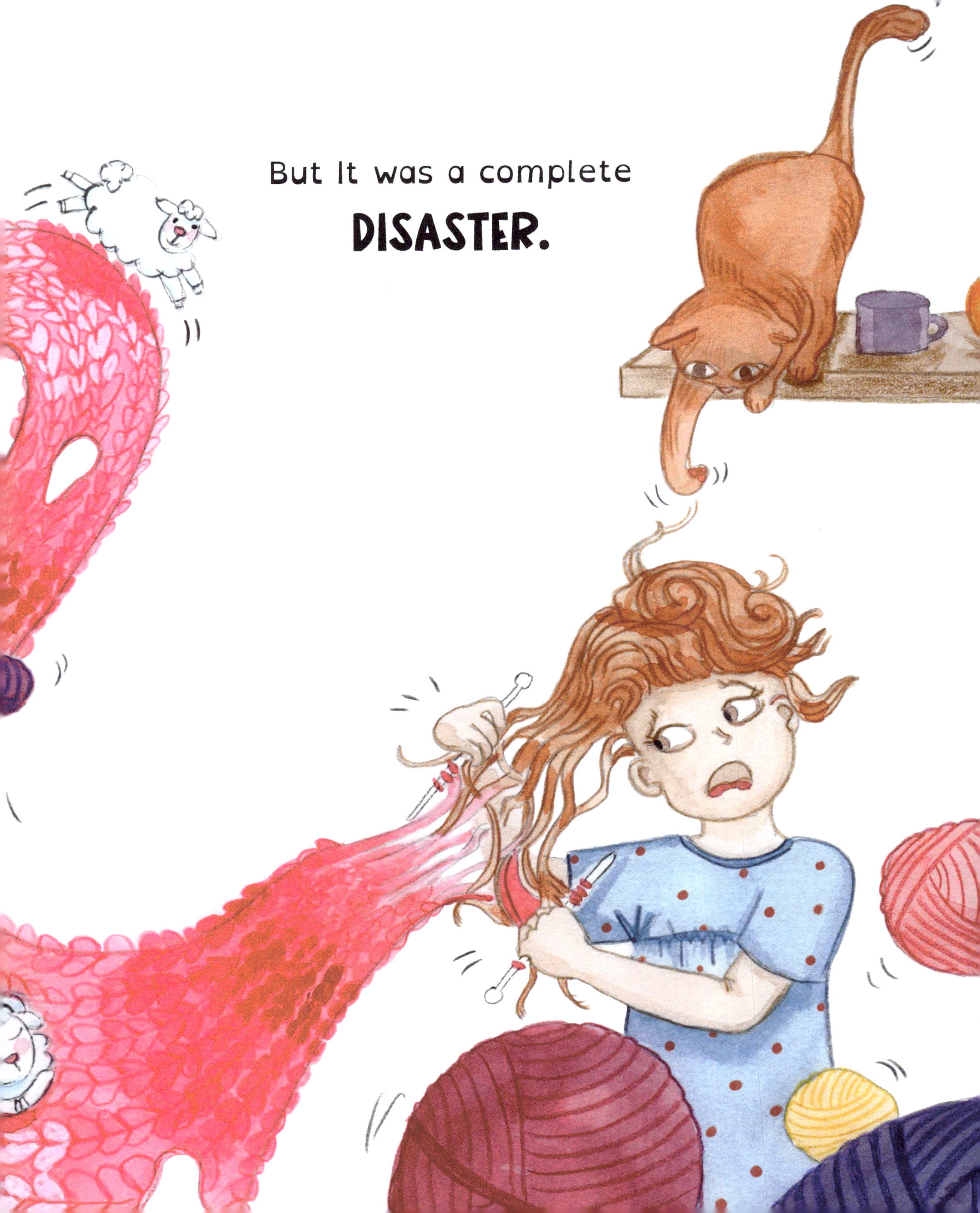

But It was a complete
DISASTER.

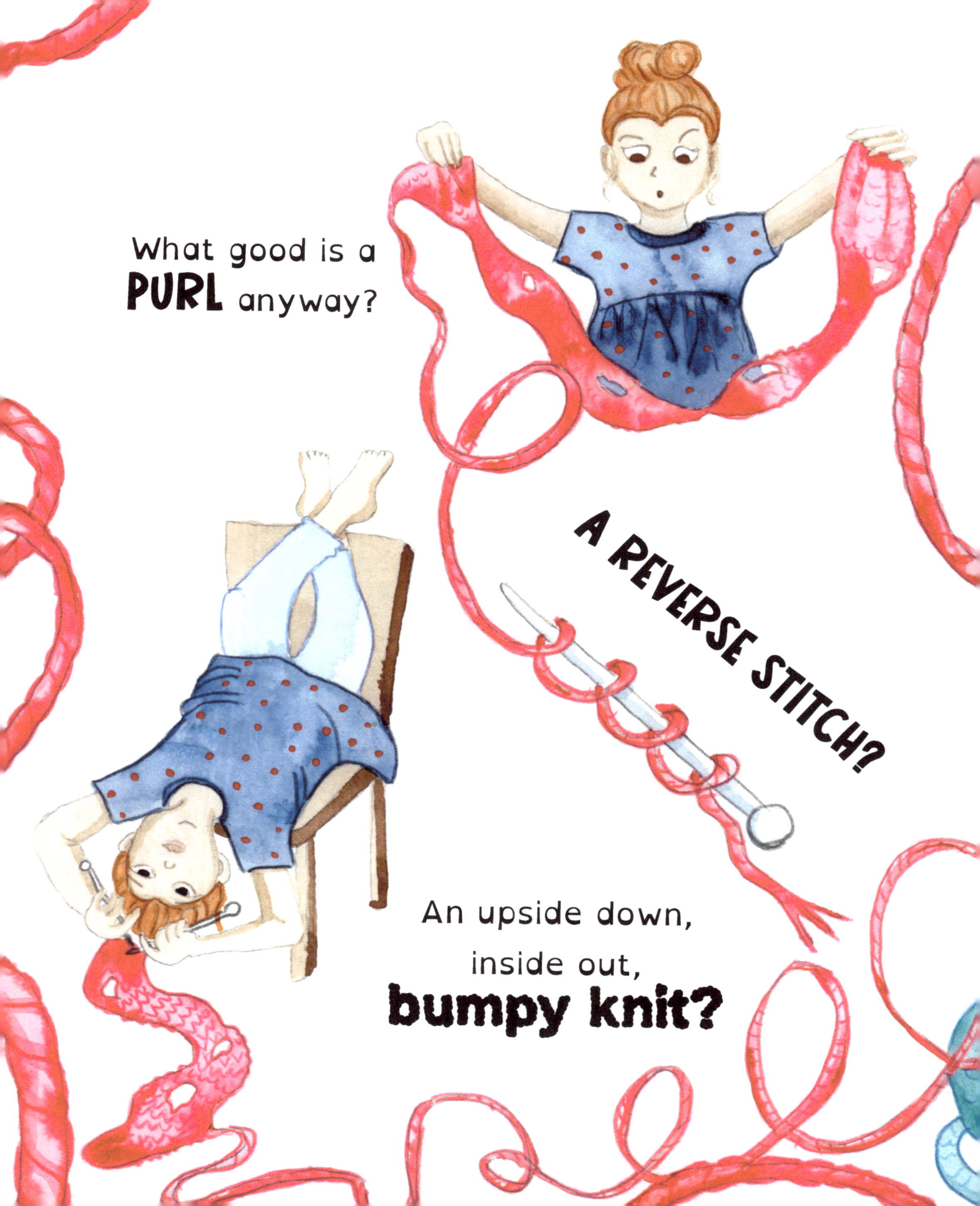

What good is a PURL anyway?
A REVERSE STITCH?
An upside down, inside out, bumpy knit?

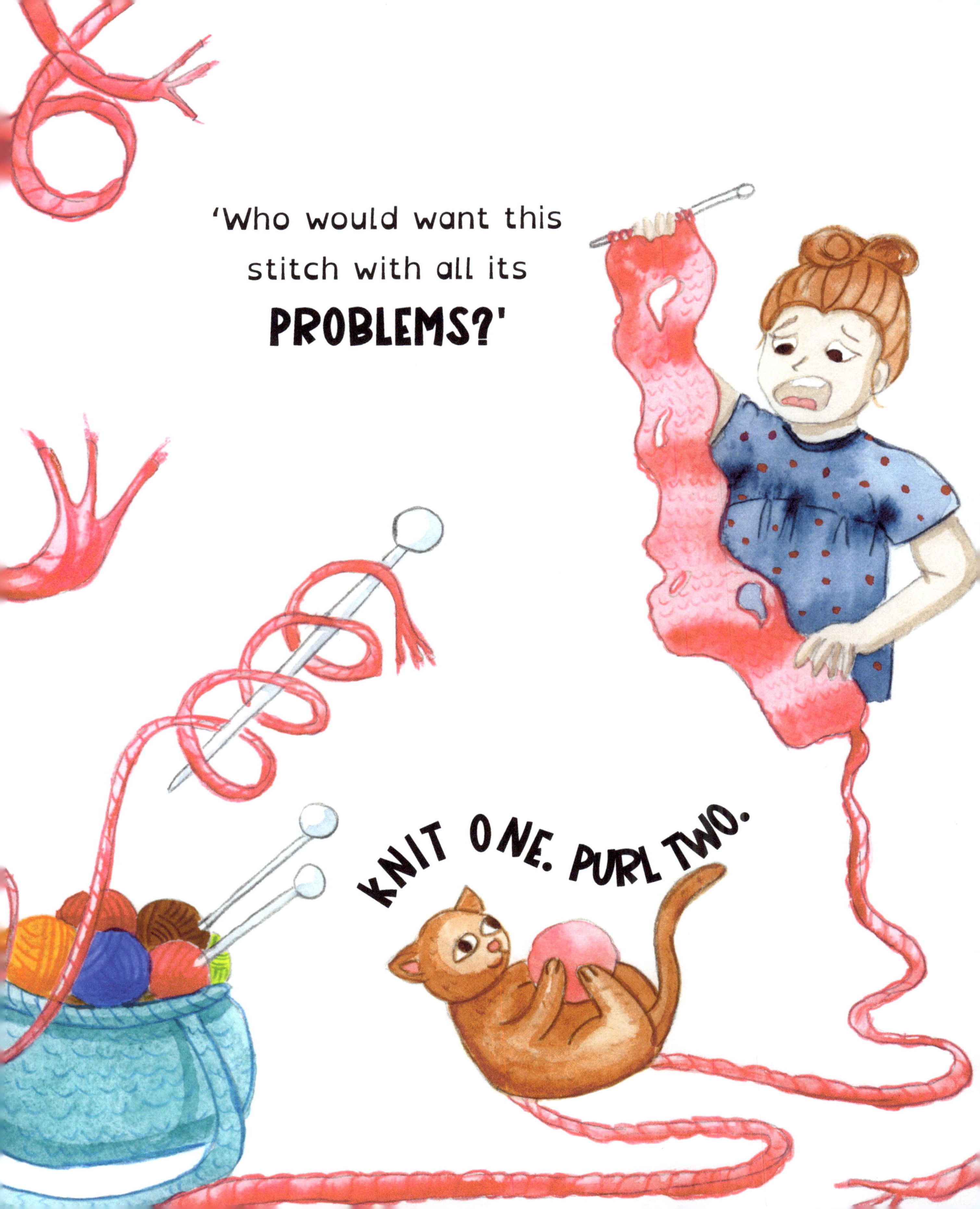

'Who would want this stitch with all its PROBLEMS?'
KNIT ONE. PURL TWO.

'Try a rug,' said Mum.
'It's **EASY**,' said Mum.

Then **inspiration** struck.

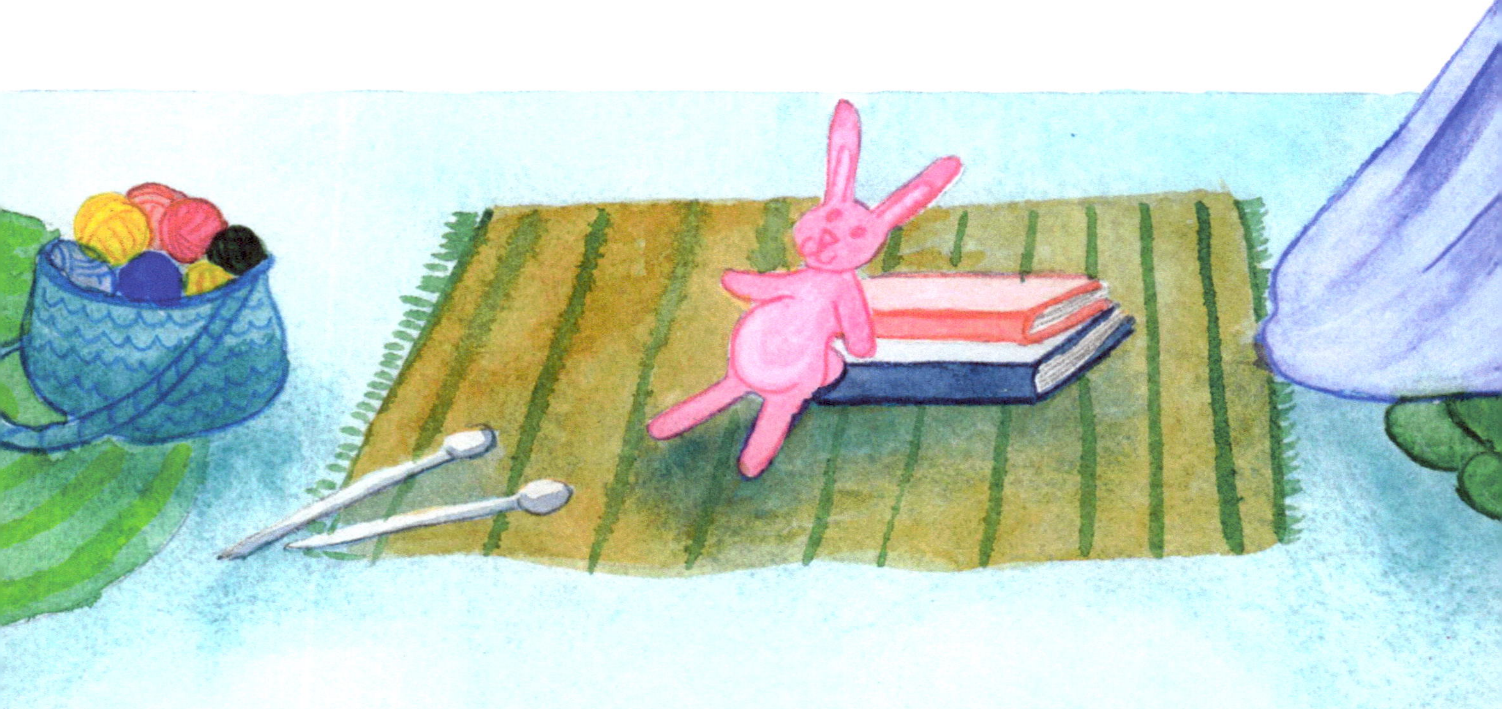

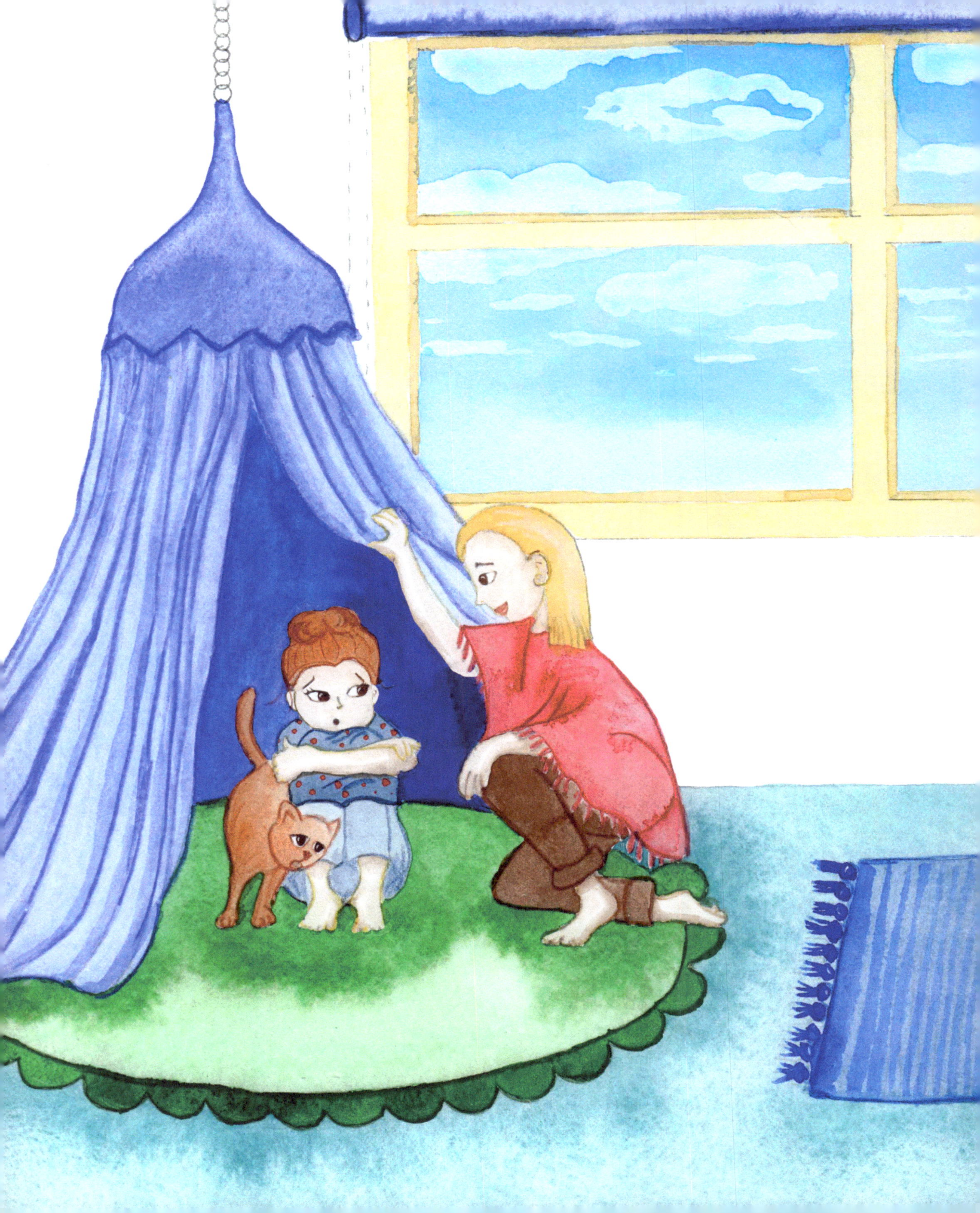

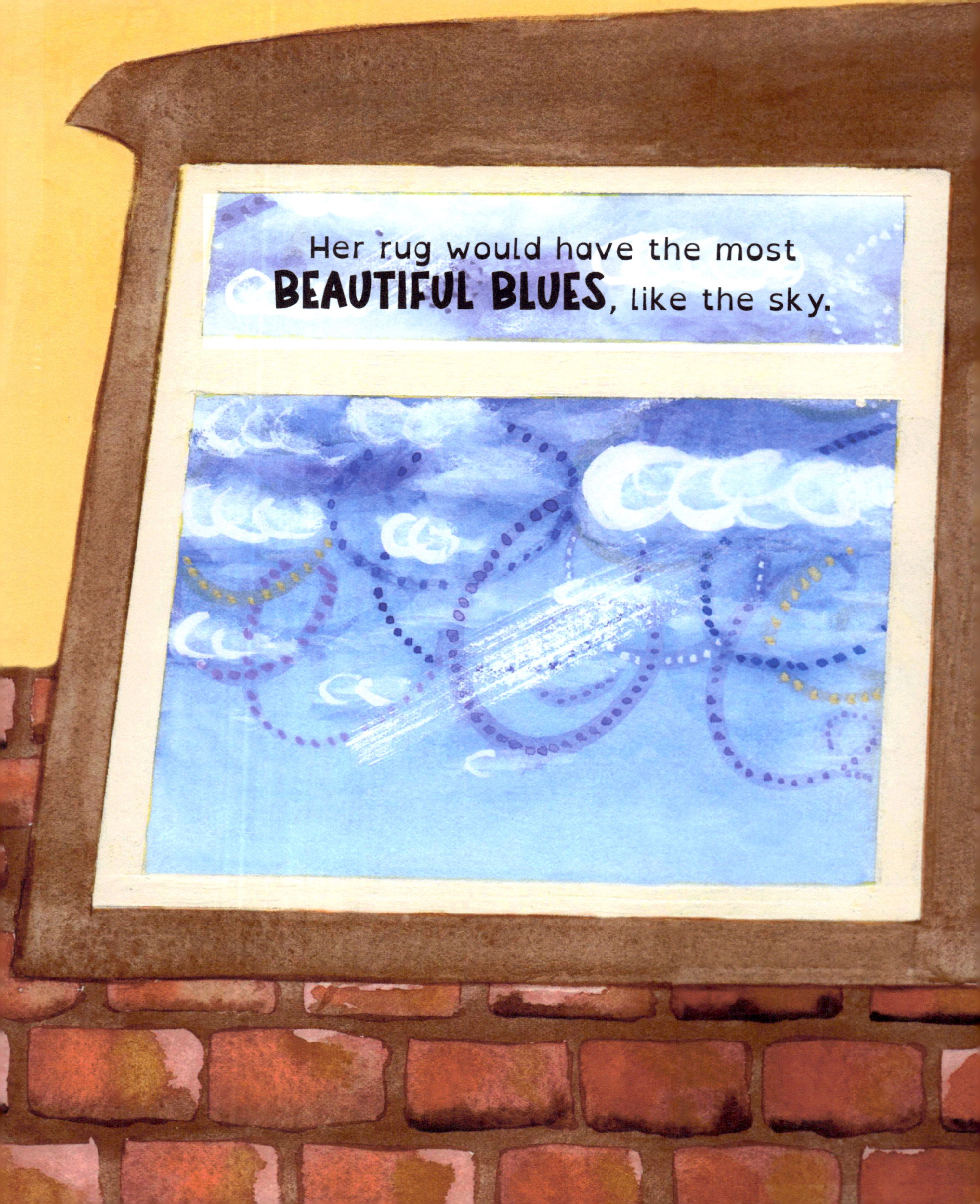

Her rug would have the most
BEAUTIFUL BLUES, like the sky.

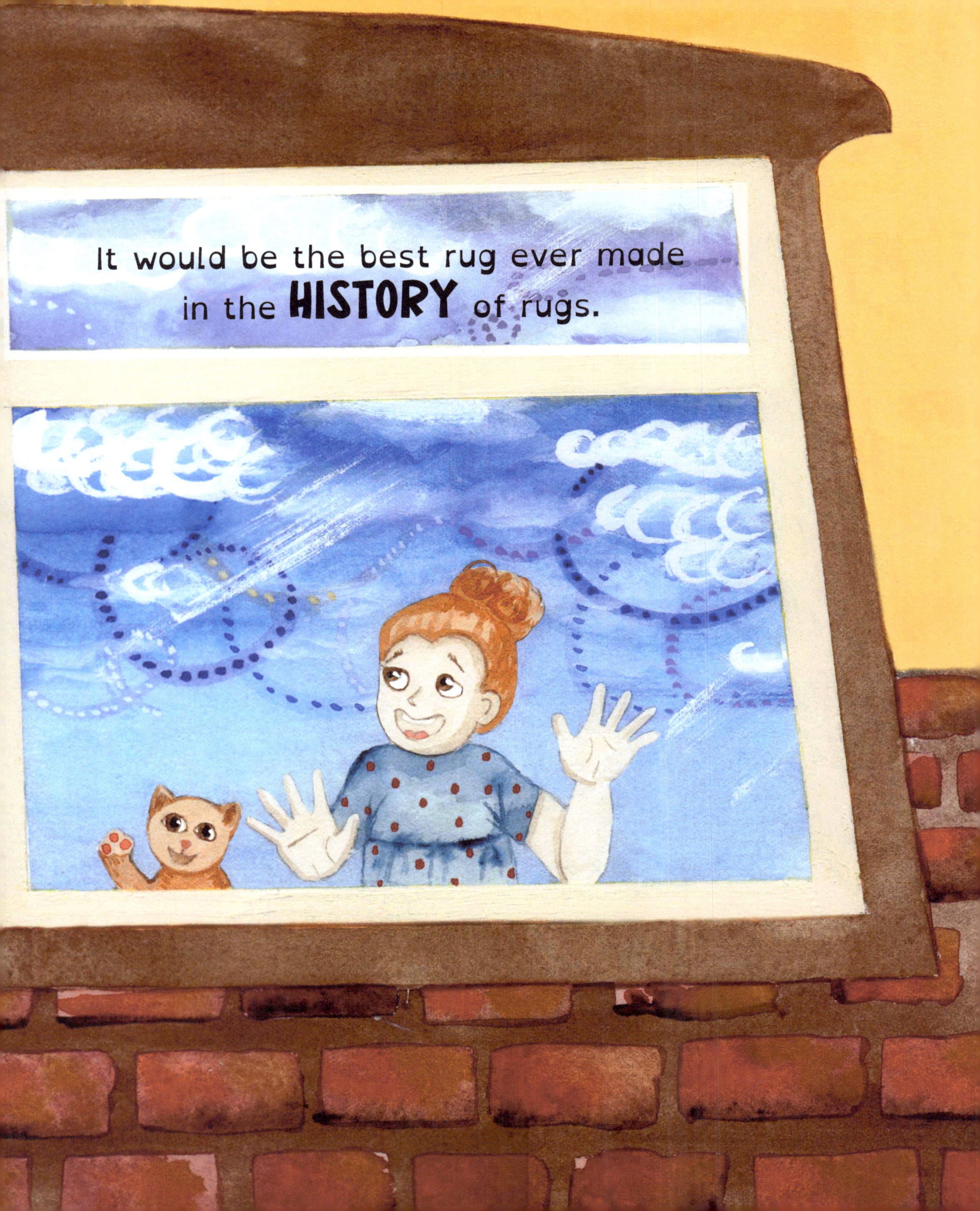It would be the best rug ever made in the HISTORY of rugs.

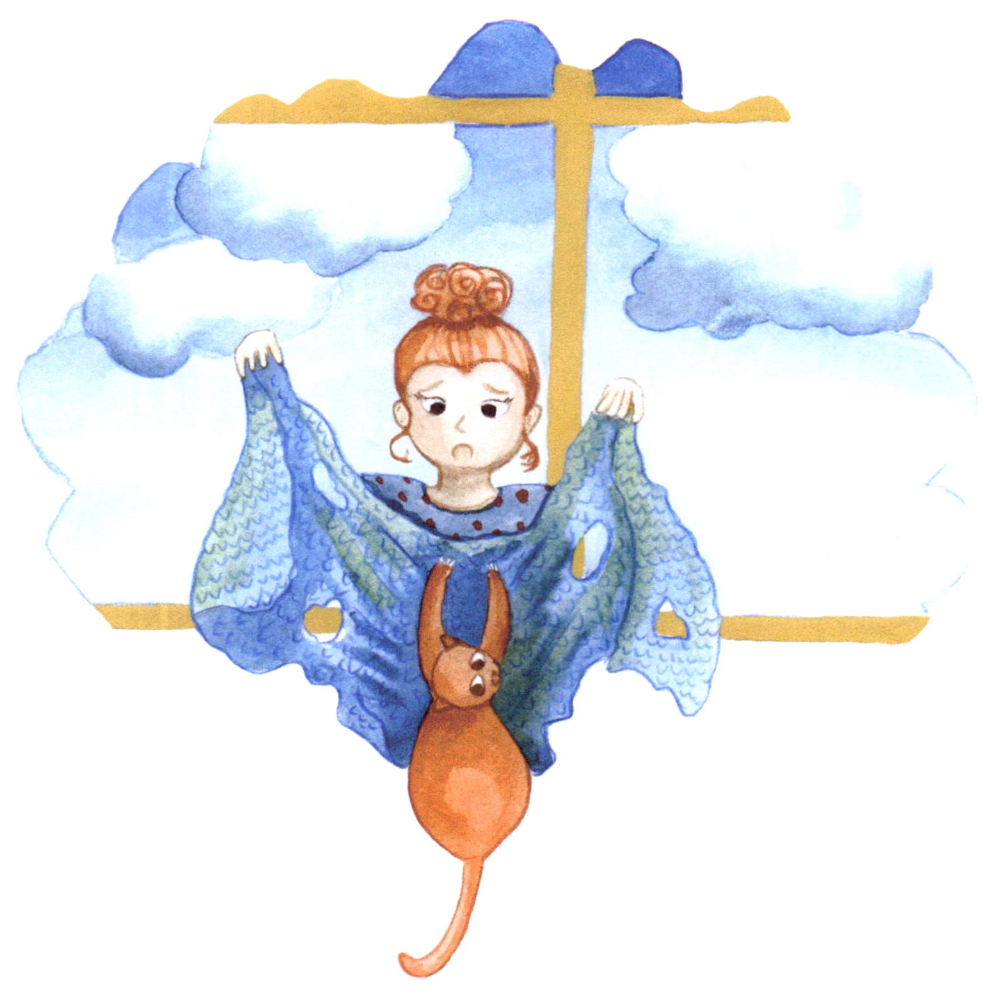

Before long, stitches were
dropped and extra ones added.
It stretched this way and that.
'It's a failure.' Yarn sighed.

The colour was sapphire,
like the deep dark ocean.
Yarn felt as **BLUE** as her rug.
'I may as well give up now.'

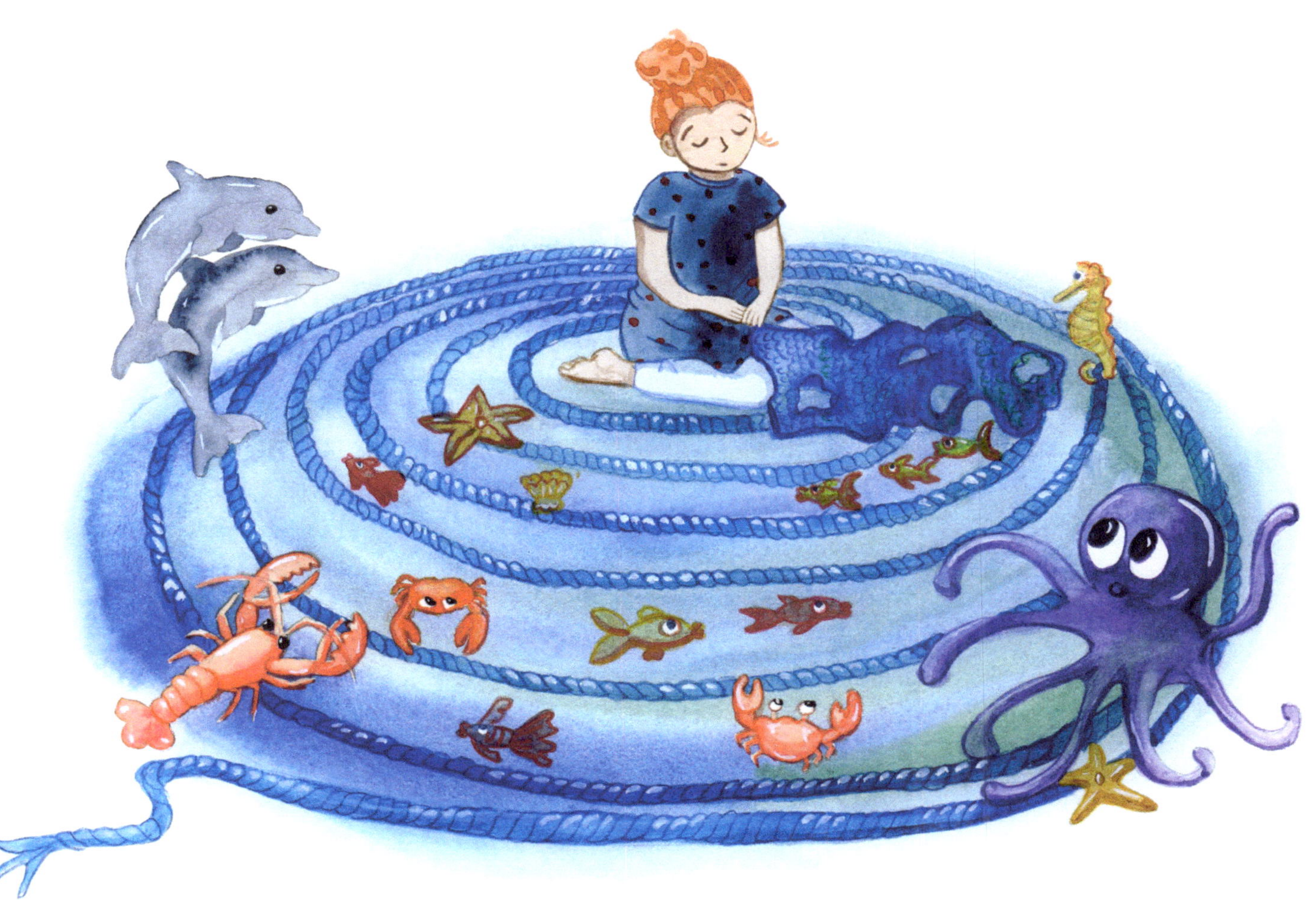

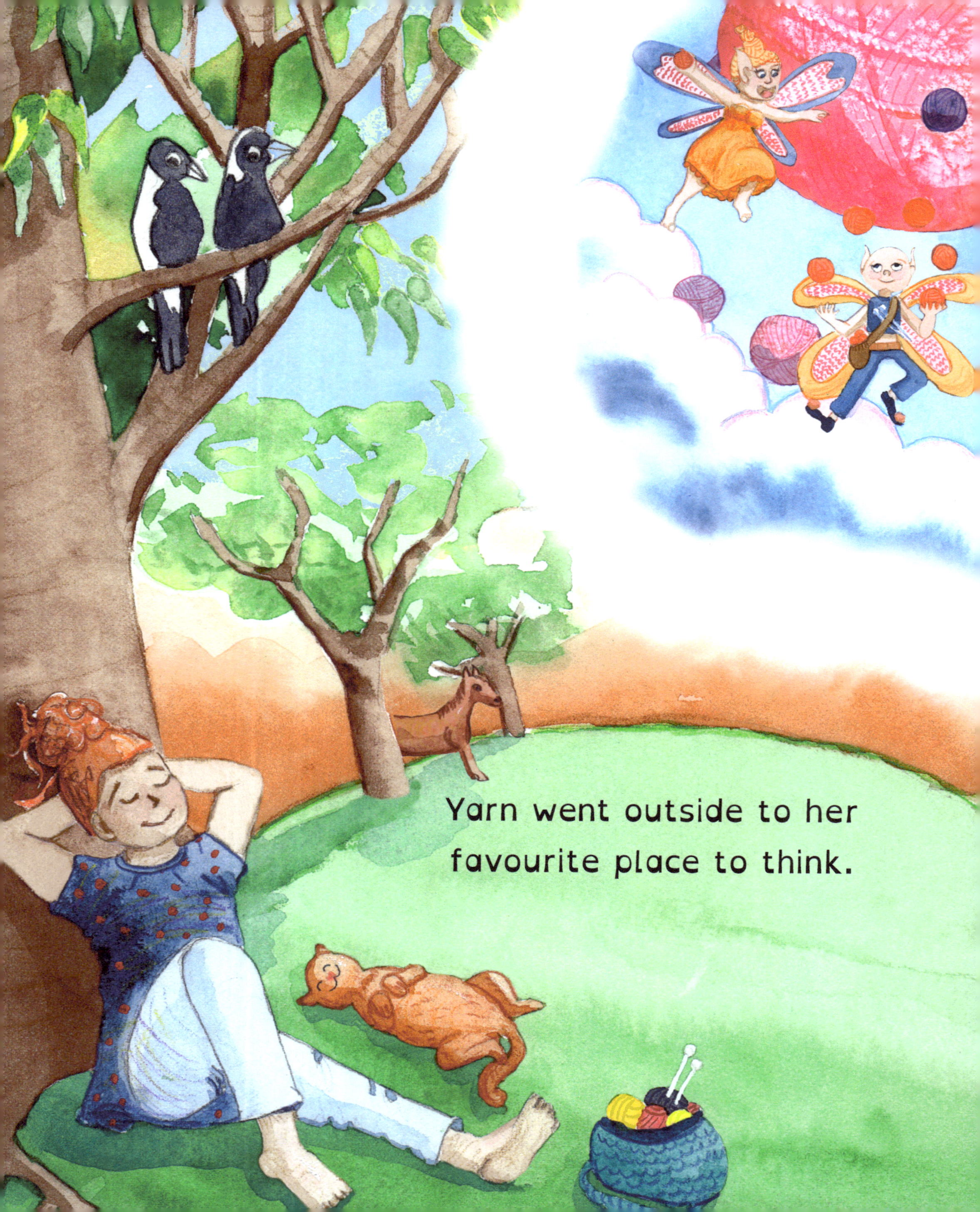

Yarn went outside to her
favourite place to think.

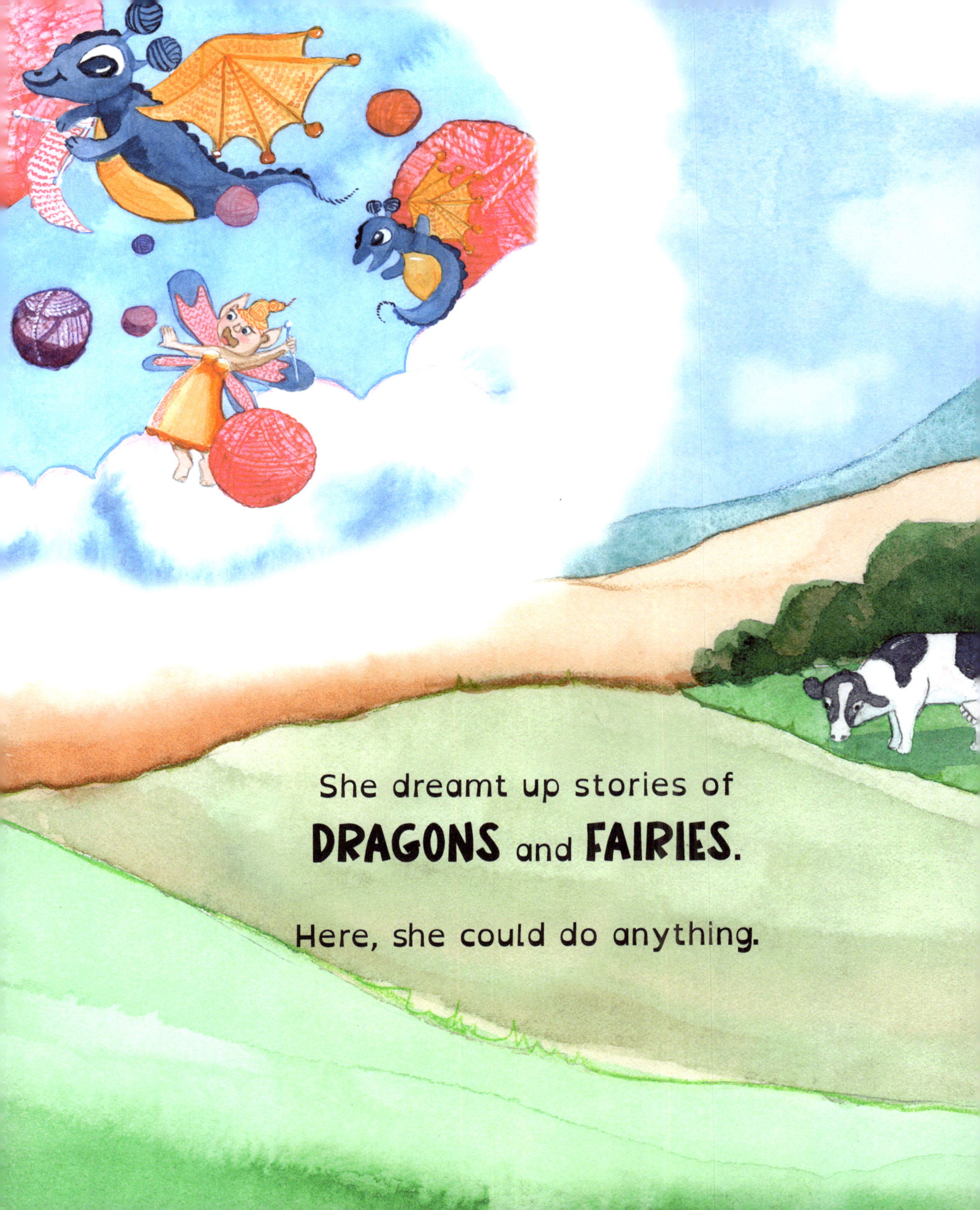

She dreamt up stories of
DRAGONS and **FAIRIES**.

Here, she could do anything.

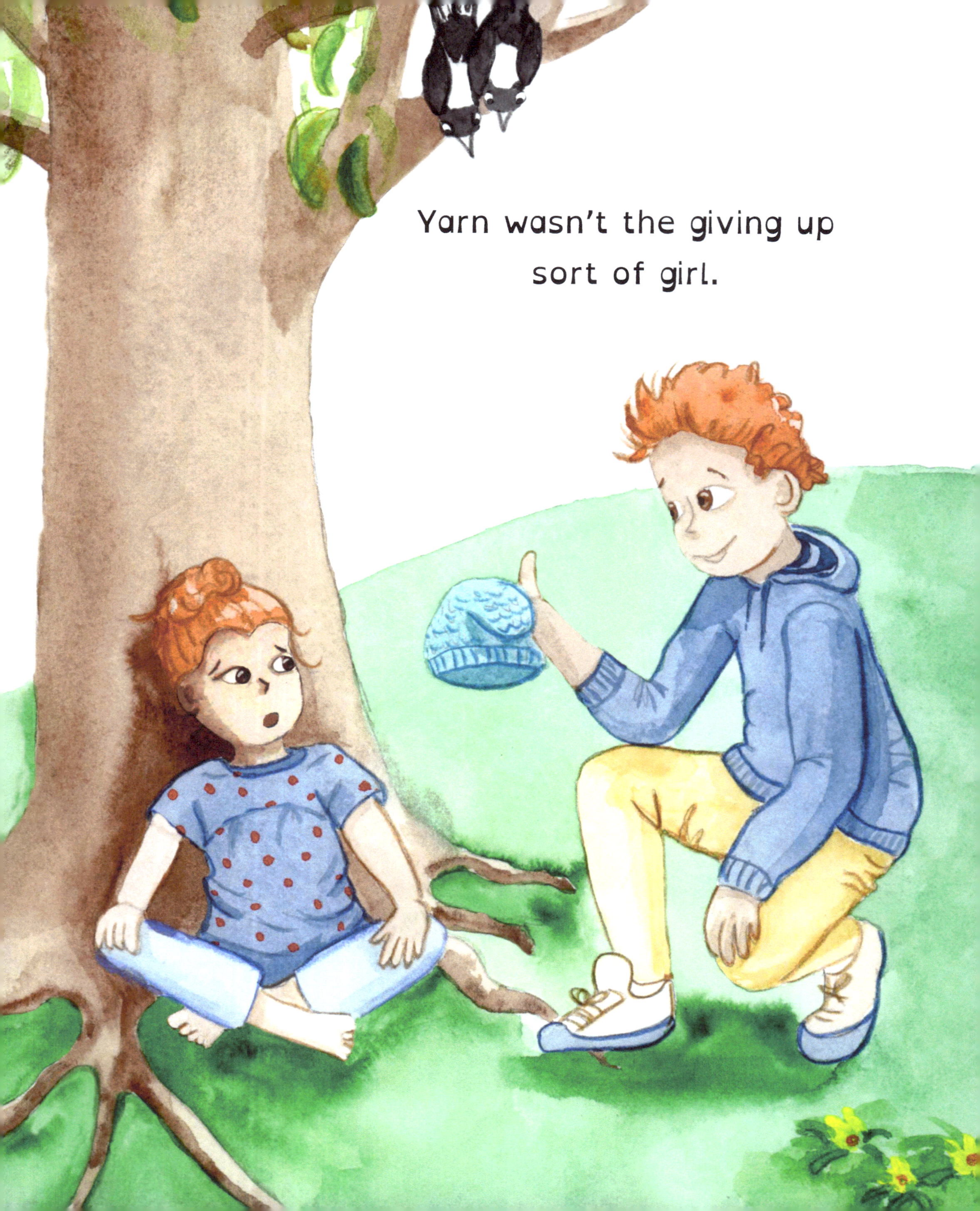

Yarn wasn't the giving up
sort of girl.

'Try a beanie,' said Freddy.
'It's **EASY**,' said Freddy.

How hard could knitting
in a circle be? She thought.

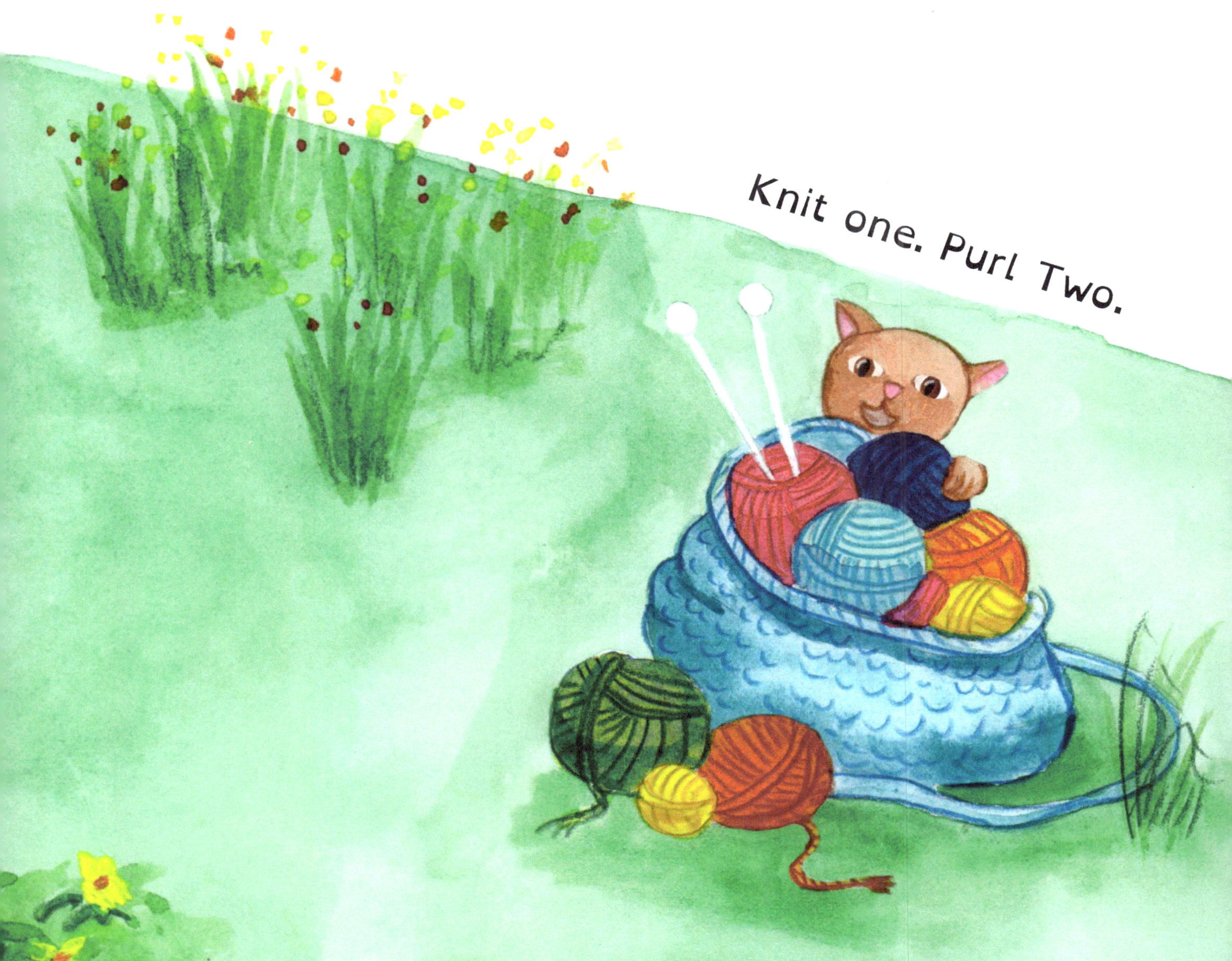

It started off easy. She knew
how to drop stitches, she was
an **EXPERT** at that.

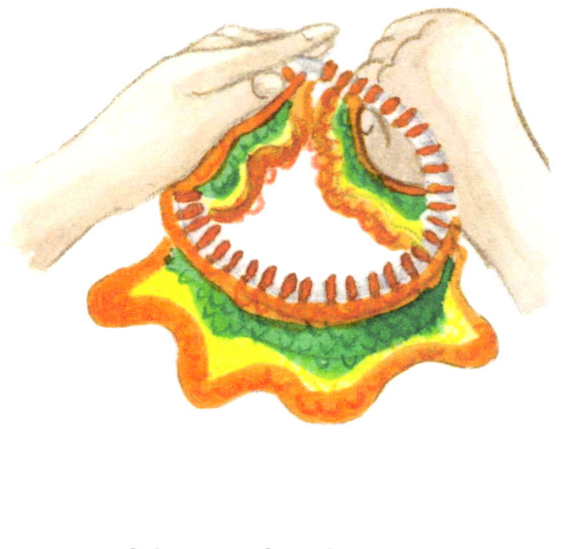

Yarn knitted
round,
and around,

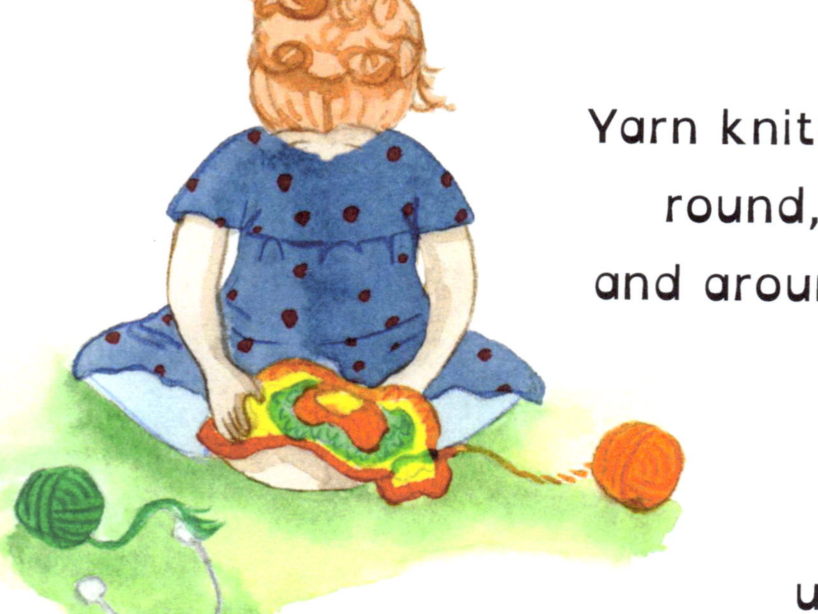

until...

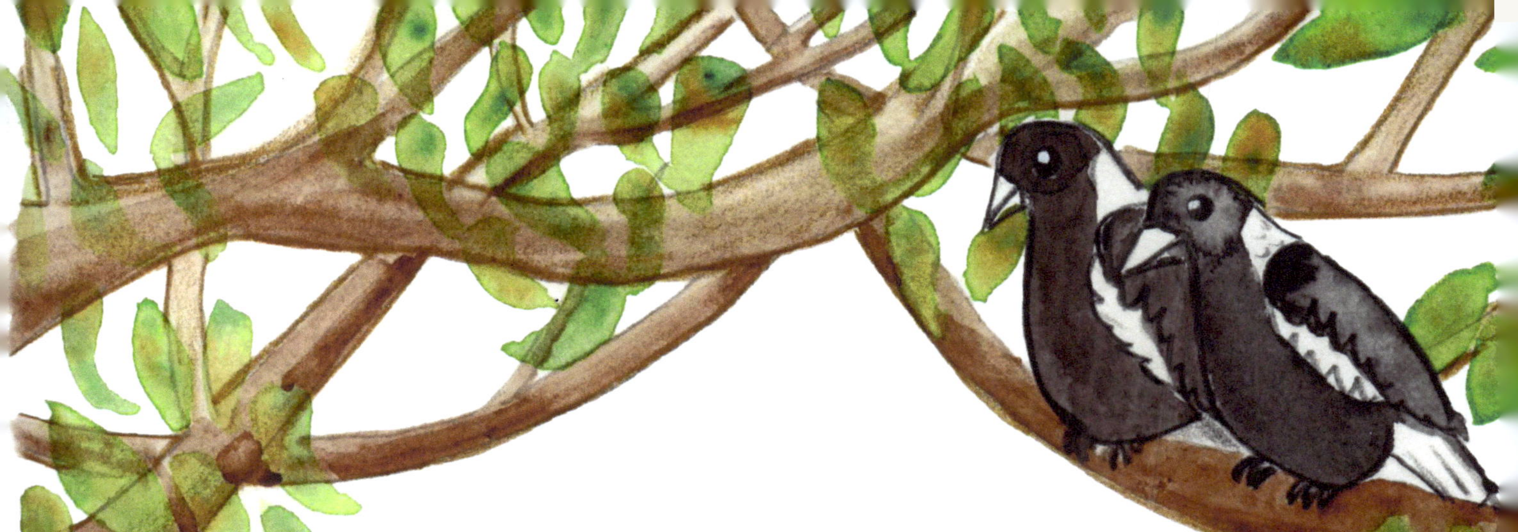

Her beanie looked like a
crazy coloured Frisbee.

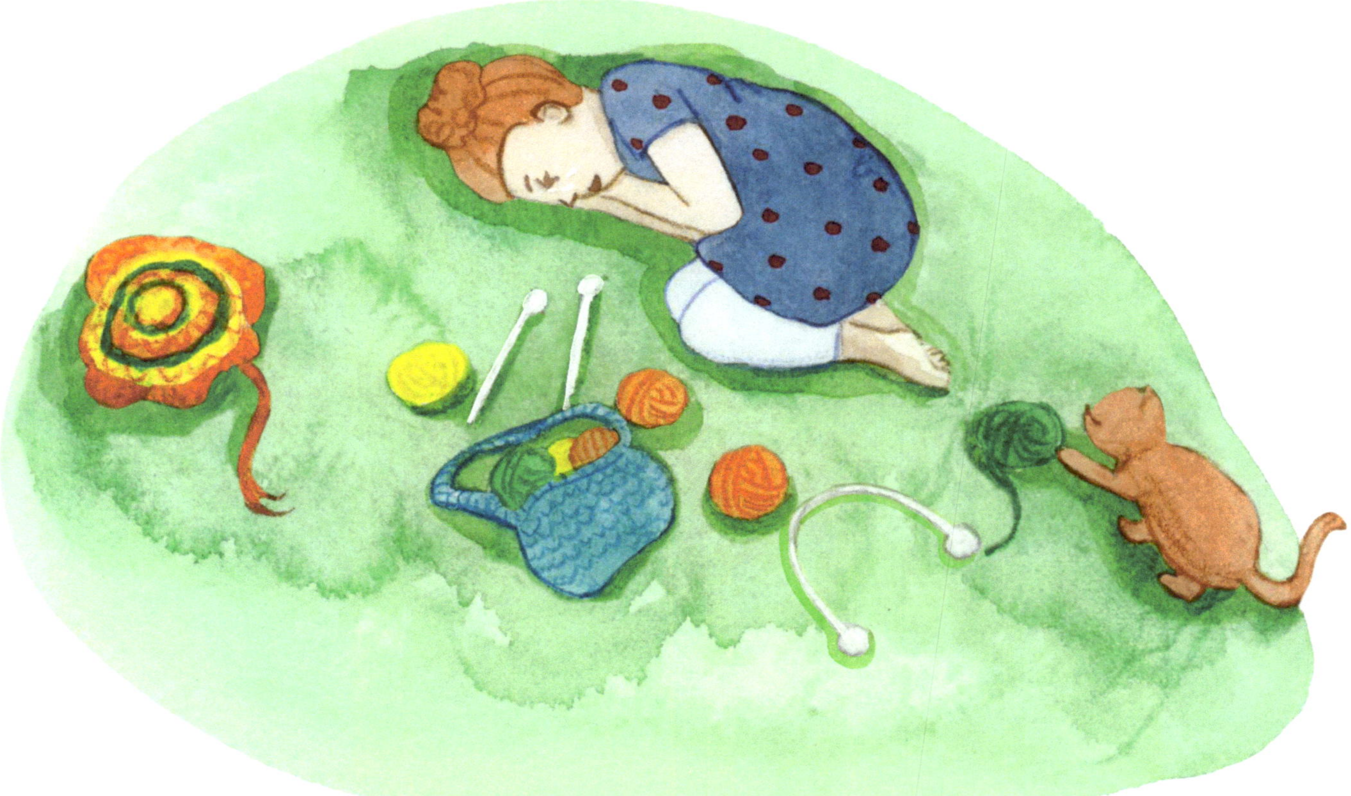

Yarn sobbed.
'It's no use. I can't knit.'

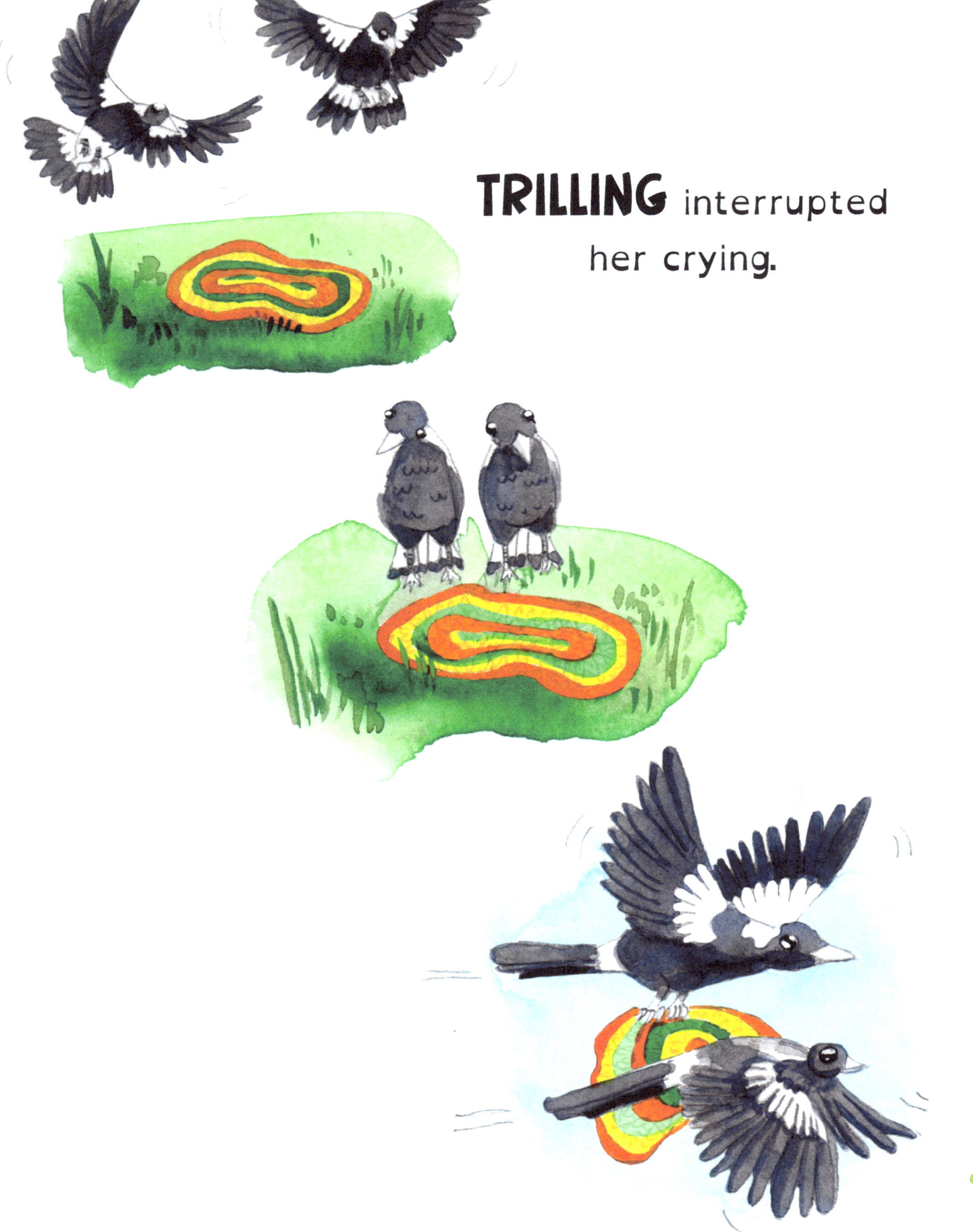

TRILLING interrupted
her crying.

Two magpies swooped up her terrible
beanie and placed it in their nest.
It was a **PERFECT** fit.

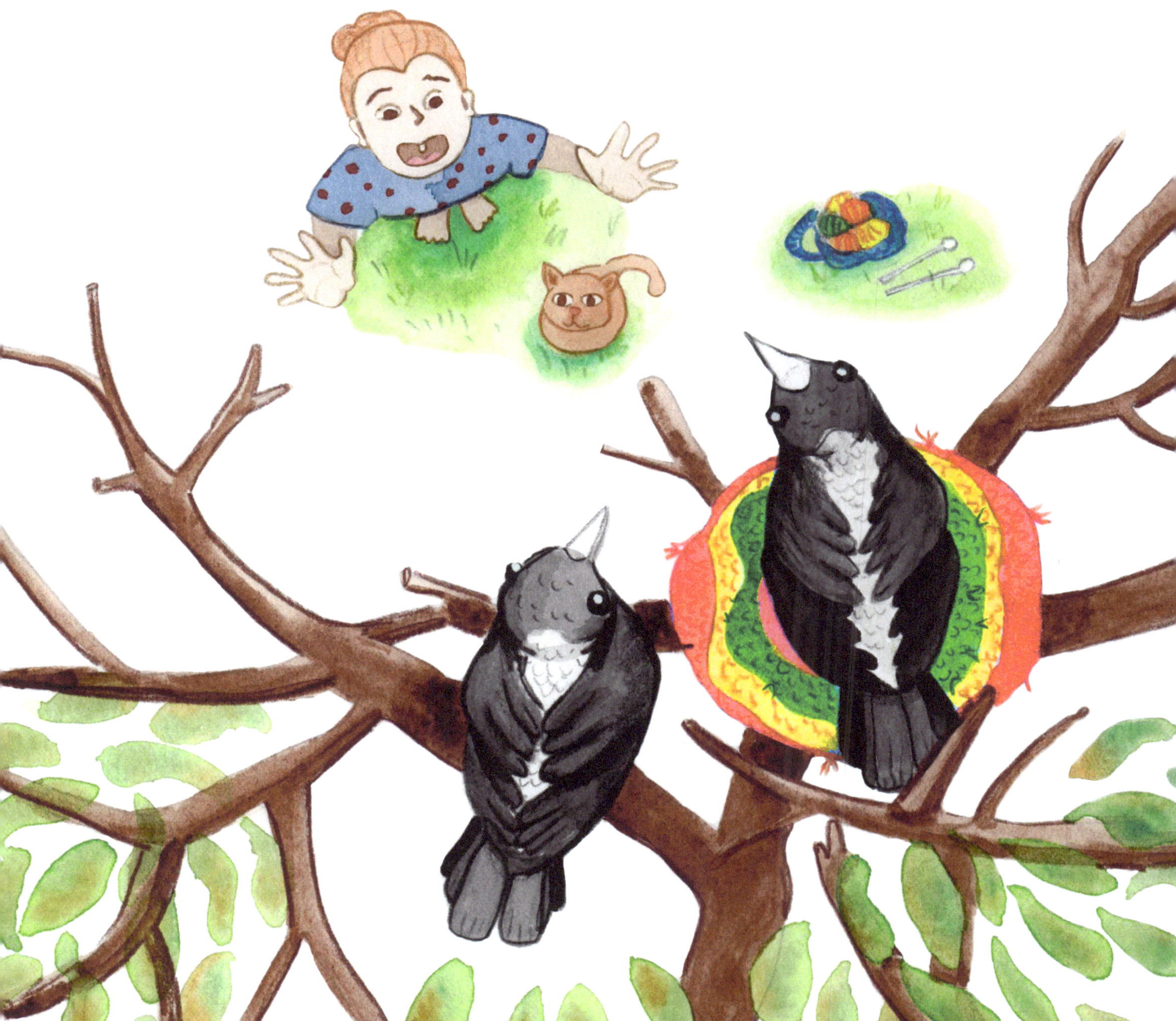

Yarn wiped away her tears
as Whinny neighed, wearing
the rug she had knitted.

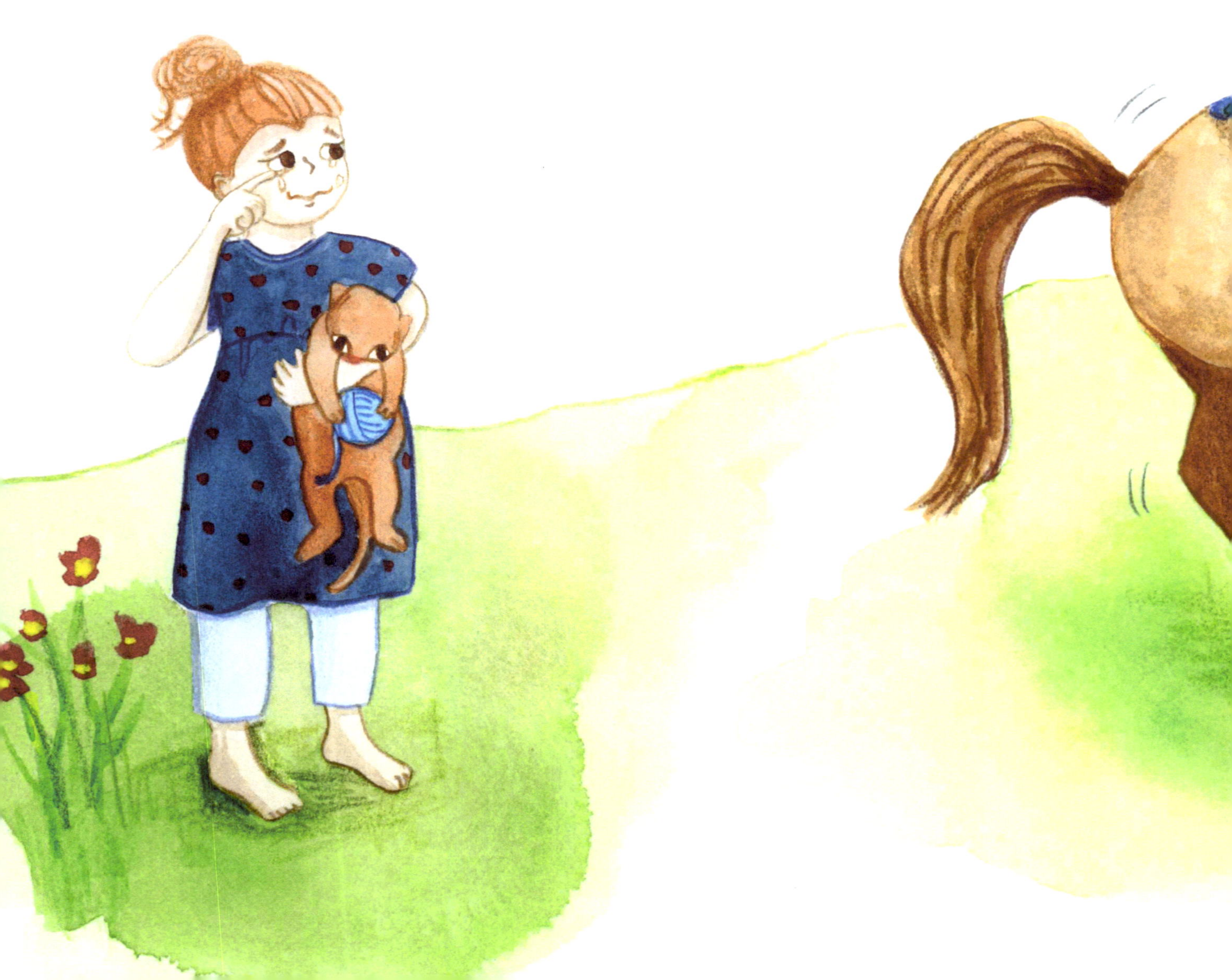

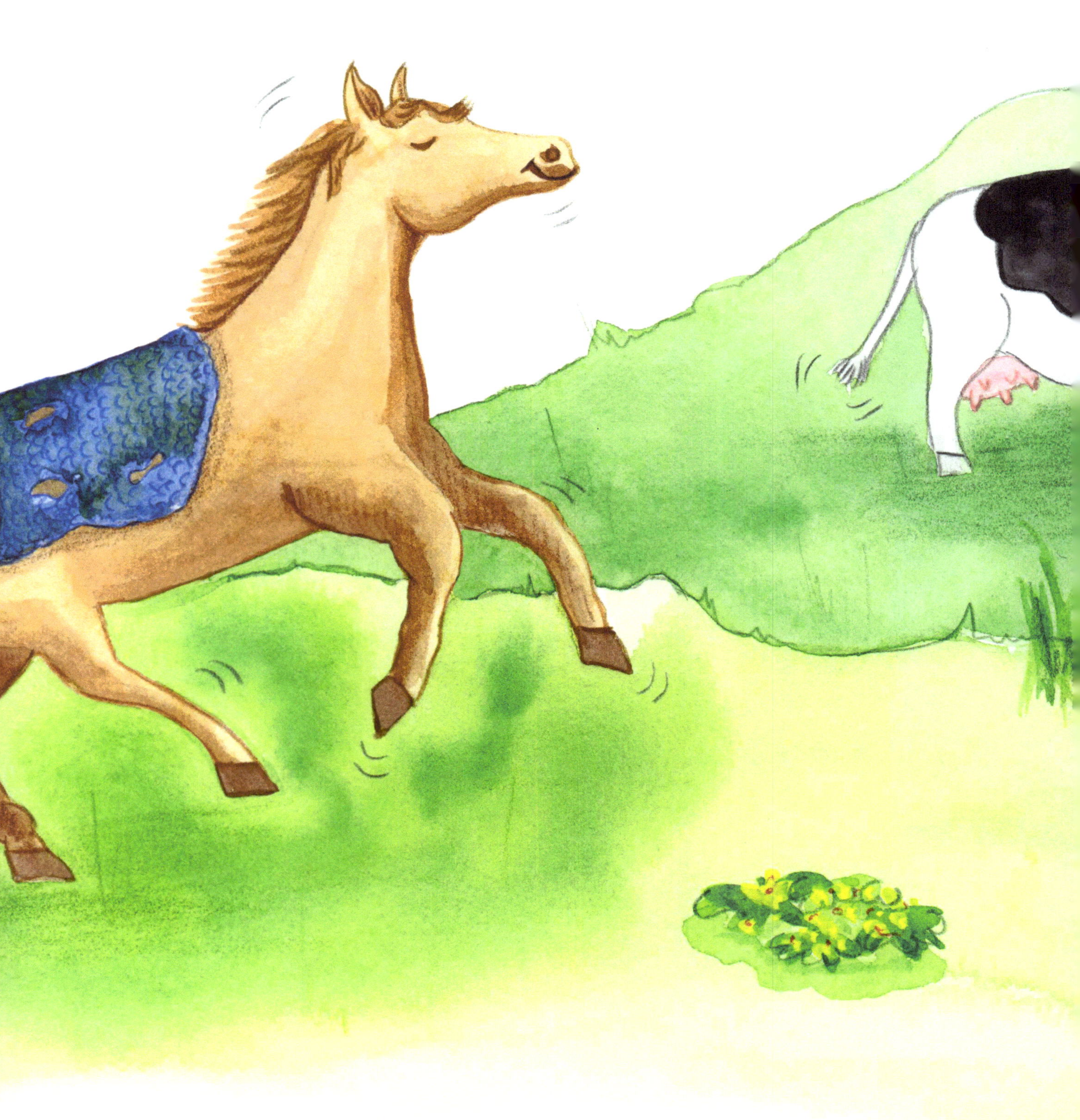

A **SMILE** returned
to Yarn's face.

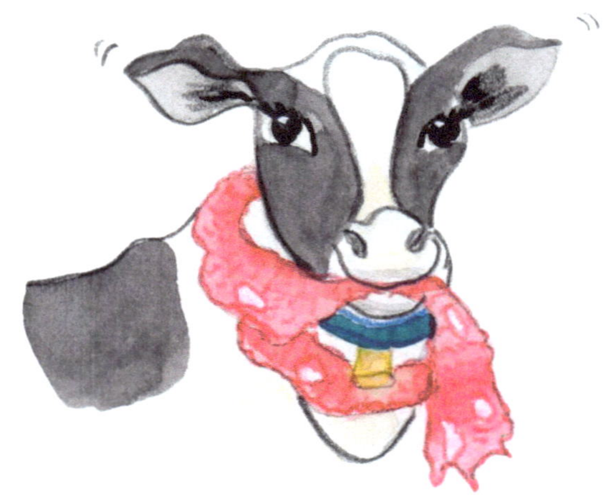

Mootilda mooed
with **HAPPINESS**
wearing her
new scarf,

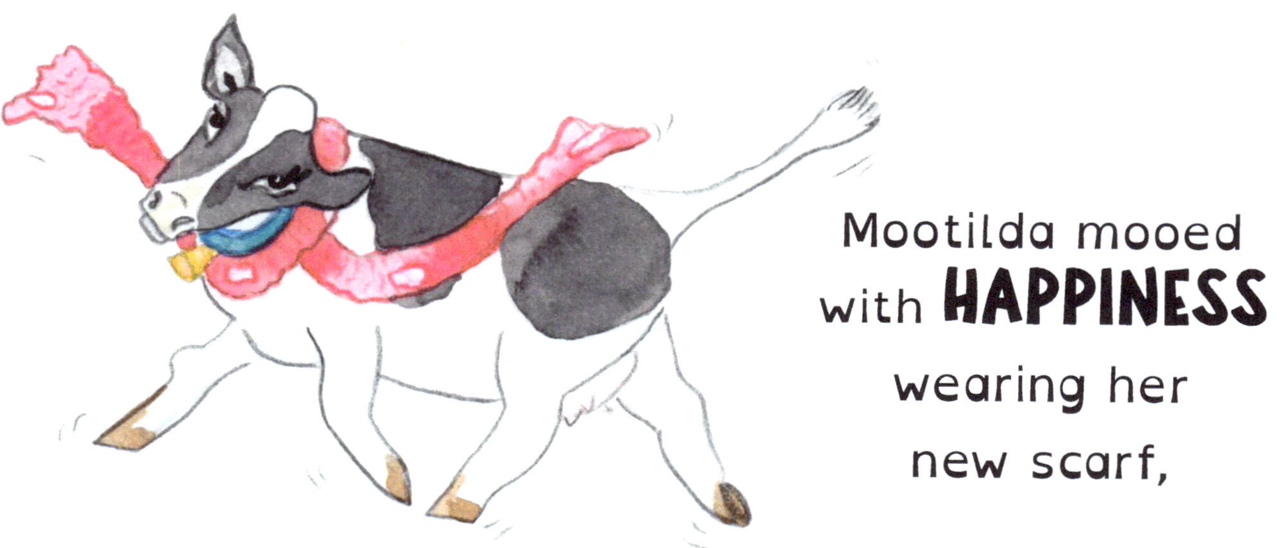

and **TONKED** her
bell in time.

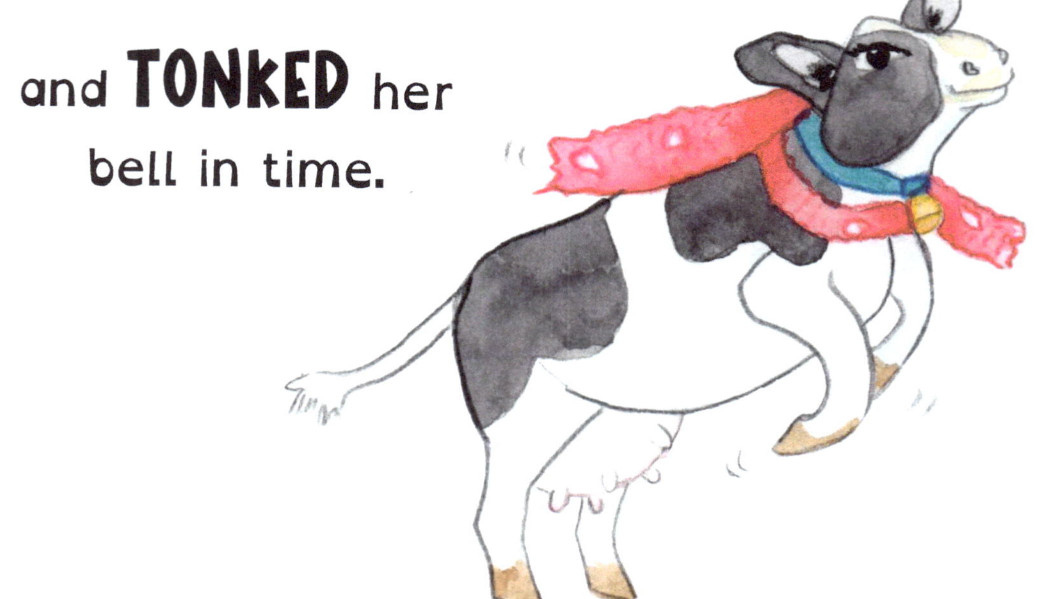

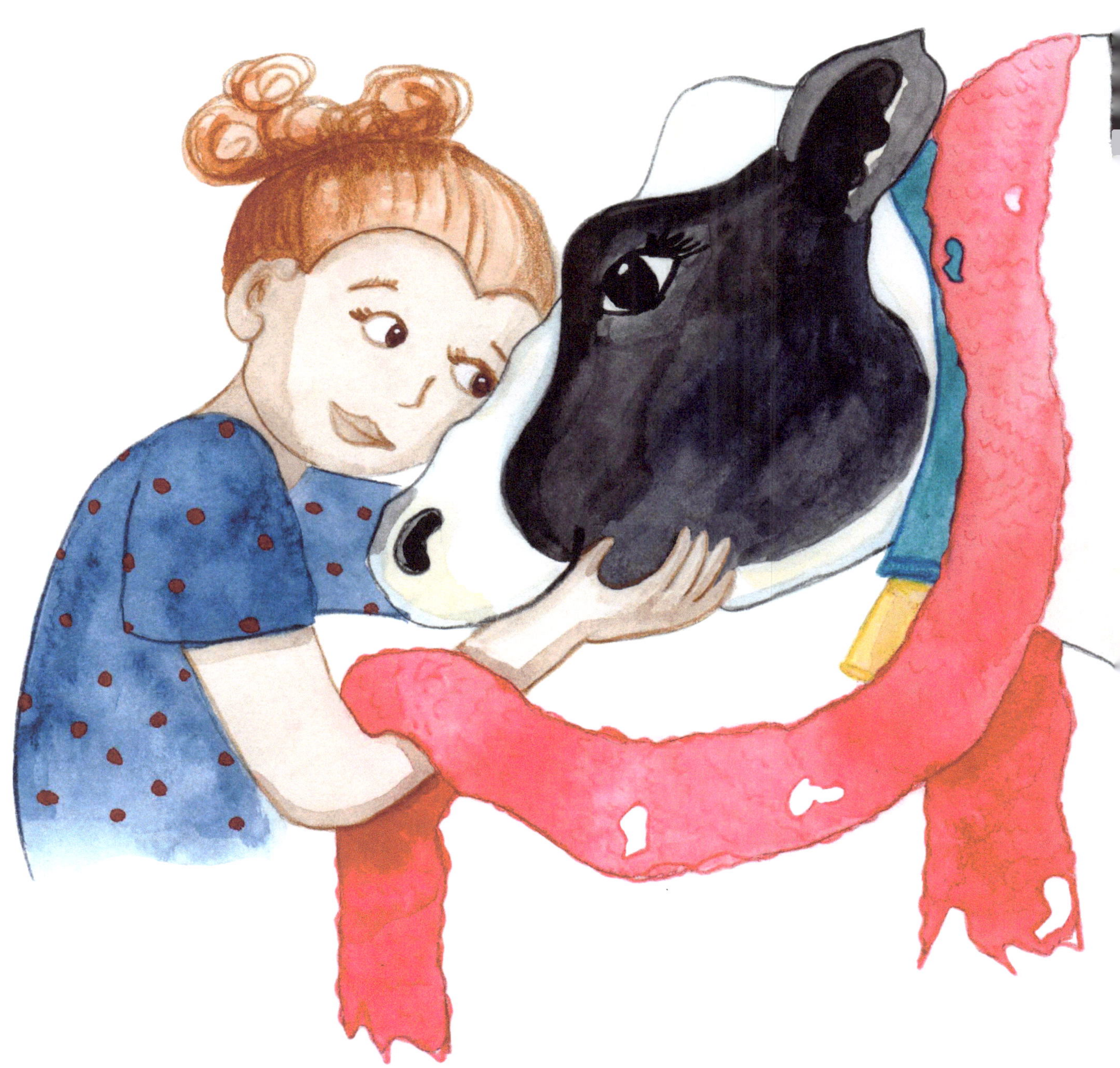

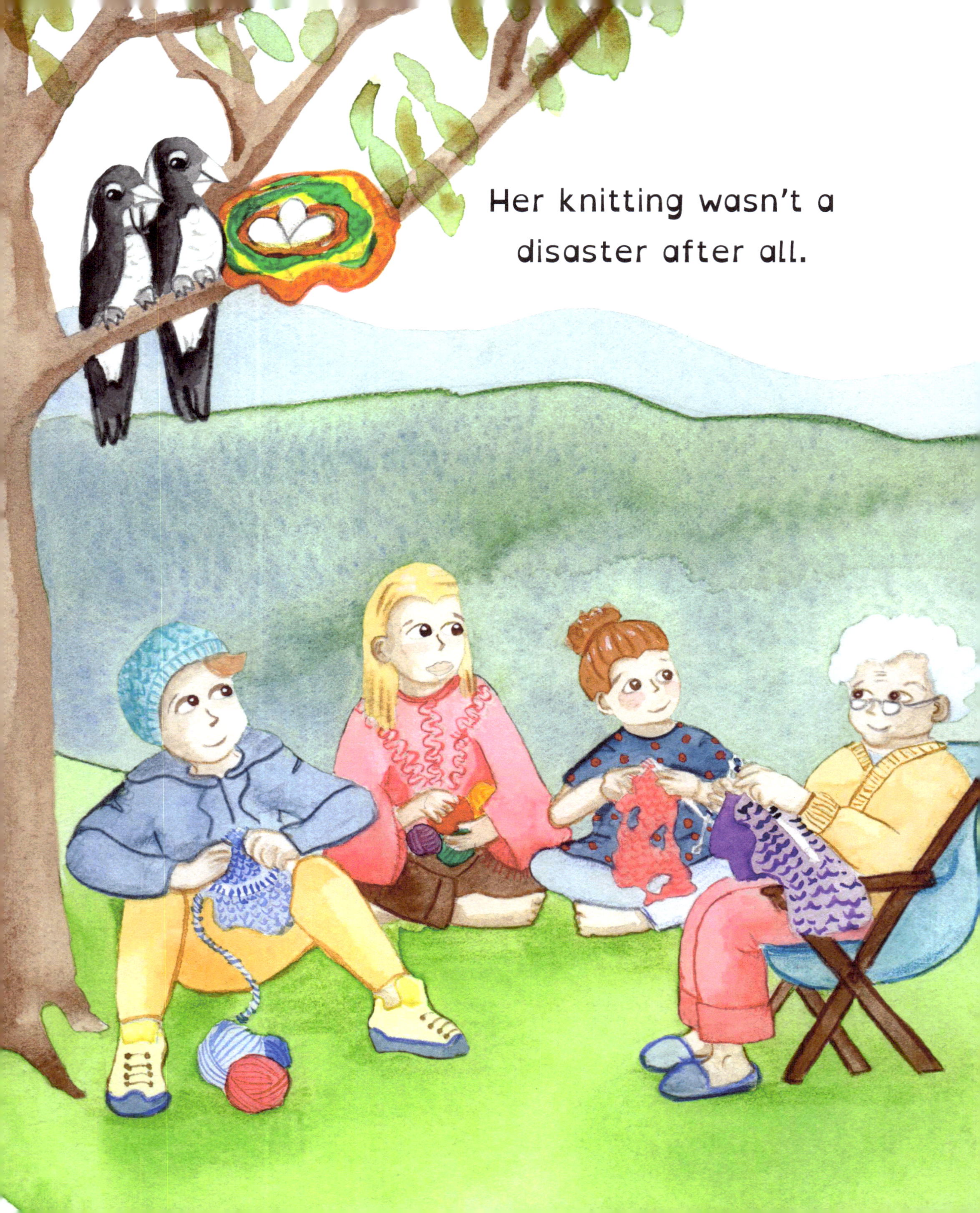

Her knitting wasn't a
disaster after all.

It was **USEFUL** and **PERFECT**.

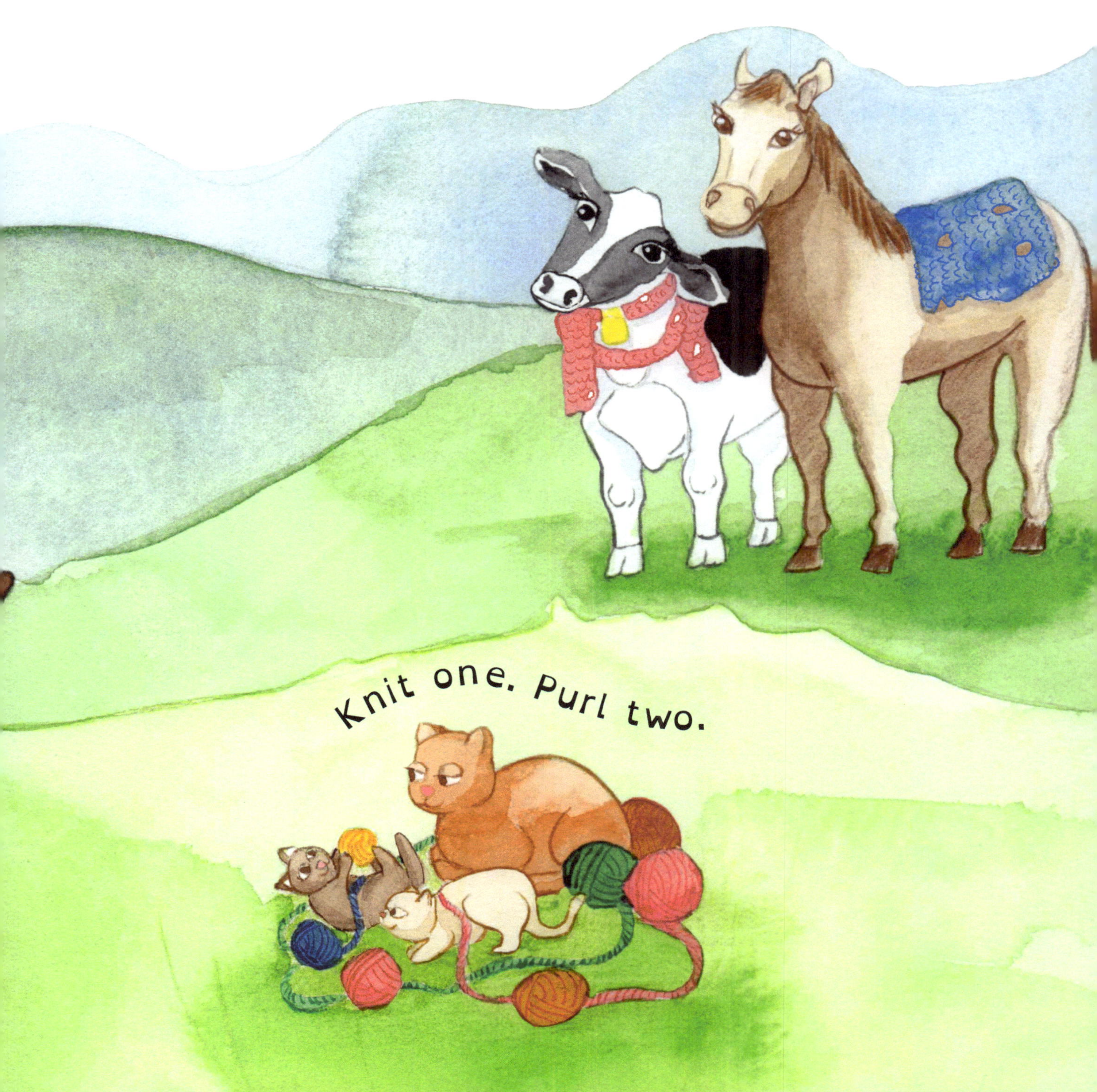

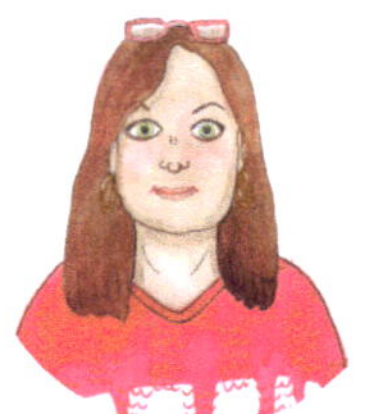

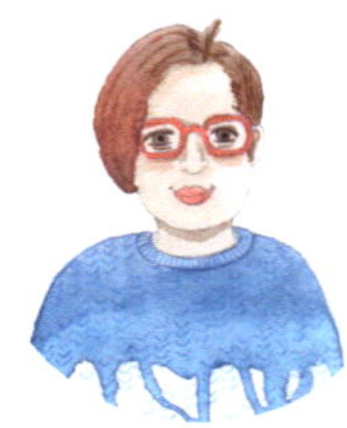

Christine Titheradge weaves captivating children's tales, leading young readers and parents on enchanting adventures. In her latest thought-provoking picture book, she invites young minds to journey towards understanding that imperfection can be beautiful and useful. Beyond her writing, Christine co-hosts the Rainforest Writing Retreat, graces as a judge for the Aurealis Awards, and finds joy in baking and spinning magical tales with her precious grandkids. Christine leaves an indelible mark on hearts and minds alike.

Yvonne Mes is a picture book author, illustrator and artist who writes for children with curious minds. She is a creative bower bird who loves exploring a variety of art materials to tell stories. She frequently speaks at festivals and schools and enjoys sharing her love of story and art with children.

You can find her at **yvonnemes.com**

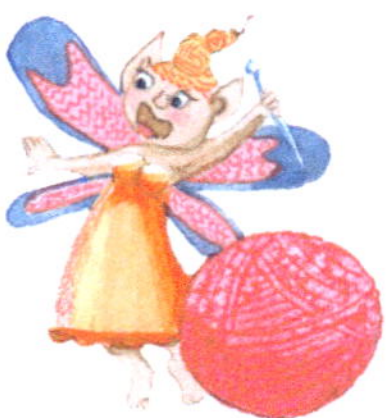

Thanks to **Charmaine Clancy**, a bright shining light, who encouraged me at every turn.

And the talented **Yvonne Mes**, who drew this story to life.

And to Samantha Wheeler for your inspiration.

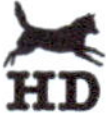 First published by Hot Doggy Press, 2023

Text copyright © Christine Titheradge, 2023
Illustration copyright © Yvonne Mes, 2023

The moral rights of the author and illustrator have been asserted.

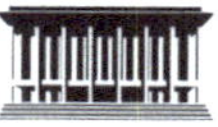 NATIONAL LIBRARY OF AUSTRALIA A catalogue record for this book is available from National Library of Australia.

ISBN: 978-0-9946245-2-9 Hardback
ISBN: 978-0-6458432-1-7 Paperback

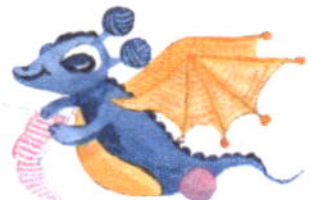

For NanMa's Grandkids - Look for the beauty in everything -

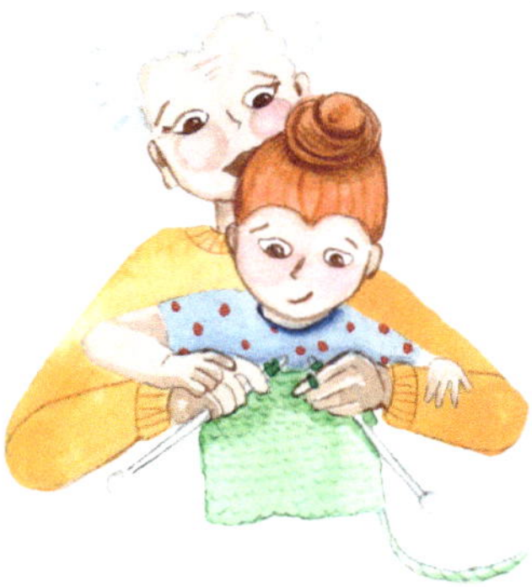